MULTICULTURAL EDUCATION SERIES

James A. Banks, Series Editor

(continued)

LITERACY ACHIEVEMENT AND DIVERSITY

Keys to Success for Students, Teachers, and Schools

Kathryn H. Au

Foreword by Patricia A. Edwards

Teachers College, Columbia University
New York and London

The author is grateful to the following organizations and publishers for granting permission to reprint revised versions of the following articles and book chapters.

Au, K. (1997). Schooling, Literacy, and Cultural Diversity in Research and Personal Experience. In A. Neumann & P. Peterson (Eds.), *Learning from Our Lives: Women, Research, and Autobiography in Education* . New York: Teachers College Press. Copyright © 1997 Teachers College Press. Reprinted with permission.

Au, K. (1998). Social Constructivism and the School Literacy Learning of Students of Diverse Cultural Backgrounds. *Journal of Literacy Research, 30*(2), 297–319. Copyright © 1998 National Reading Conference/Literacy Research Association.

Au, K. (2007). Culturally Responsive Instruction: Application to Multiethnic Classrooms. *Pedagogies: An International Journal, 2*(1), 1–18. Copyright © 2007 Taylor and Francis. Reprinted with permission.

Au, K. (2008). If Can, Can: Hawai'i Creole and Reading Achievement. *Educational Perspectives 41*(1), 66–76. Copyright © 2007 College of Education, University of Hawai'i. Reprinted with permission.

Au, K. (1997). Ownership, Literacy Achievement, and Students of Diverse Cultural Backgrounds. In J. Guthrie & A. Wigfield (Eds.), *Reading Engagement: Motivating Readers Through Integrated Instruction*. Washington, DC: International Reading Association. Copyright © 1997 International Reading Association. Reprinted with permission.

Au, K. (2003). Balanced Literacy Instruction: Implications for Students of Diverse Backgrounds. In J. Flood, D. Lapp, J. Squire, & J. Jensen (Eds.), *Handbook of Research on Teaching the English Language Arts* (2nd Ed.). New York: Erlbaum and Taylor and Francis. Copyright ©2003 Erlbaum/Taylor and Francis. Reprinted with permission.

Au, K. (2005). Negotiating the Slippery Slope: School Change and Literacy Achievement. *Journal of Literacy Reserach, 37*(3), 267–286. Copyright ©2005 National Reading Conference/Literacy Research Association. Reprinted with permission.

Published by Teachers College Press, 1234 Amsterdam Avenue, New York, NY 10027

Library of Congress Cataloging-in-Publication Data

Au, Kathryn H., 1947–
    Literacy achievement and diversity : keys to success for students, teachers, and schools / Kathryn H. Au.
        p. cm.— (Multicultural education series)
    Includes bibliographical references and index.
    ISBN 978-0-8077-5206-7 (pbk. : alk. paper)
    ISBN 978-0-8077-5207-4 (hardcover : alk. paper)
    1. Language arts—Social aspects—United States. 2. Literacy—Social aspects—United States. 3. Multicultural education—United States. 4. School improvement programs—United States. I. Title.
    LB1576.A88 2011
    370.1170973—dc22   2010051918

ISBN 978-0-8077-5206-7 (paper)
ISBN 978-0-8077-5207-4 (hardcover)

Printed on acid-free paper
Manufactured in the United States of America

18   17   16   15   14   13   12   11   8   7   6   5   4   3   2   1

Contents

122941

Series Foreword

Explanations for disparities in the academic achievement of low-income, minority, and mainstream students have a long, complex, and contested history in the United States and other nations (Banks, 2004, 2009). President Lyndon B. Johnson's War on Poverty, initiated by legislation introduced in 1964, focused attention on the nation's poor, including vulnerable students in the public schools (Harrington, 1962). In the 1960s, the institutional explanation for the poor academic achievement of students from low-income and ethnic minority groups was centered on genetics. Liberal social scientists and educators constructed the cultural deprivation paradigm to provide an alternative to the genetic explanation that was embedded and largely uncontested in American institutions, including the schools, colleges, and universities.

The cultural deprivation explanation—which must be understood within its historical, cultural, and political context—was proposed by progressive social scientists such as Benjamin C. Bloom, Allison Davis, and Robert Hess (1965), who were on the faculty of the highly esteemed education department at the University of Chicago. The cultural deprivation explanation views the limited cultural capital in the home and communities of low-income and minority students as the major factor that explains their low academic achievement. It devotes little attention to other factors, such as the political economy of the larger society or the structures within the school. Consequently, the cultural deprivation explanation, as Ryan (1971) cogently argues, was widely viewed as "blaming the victims" for their dismal educational status and structural exclusion.

The cultural deficit explanation still casts a long shadow on the American educational landscape. It has been internalized by many teachers, resulting in low teacher expectations and uninspiring teaching in many inner-city classrooms populated heavily by African American and Latino students (Green, 2009). A group of pioneering scholars constructed the cultural difference paradigm in the 1970s and 1980s to critique and provide an alternative to the cultural deficit explanation. These scholars included Manuel Ramírez and Aflredo Castañeda (1974), Ronald Edmonds (1986), and A. Wade Boykin (1986).

The cultural difference paradigm provides a significant antidote to the cultural deficit explanation and reveals the strengths and resilience of the families, communities, and cultures of students from diverse racial, ethnic, and linguistic groups (Wang & Gordon, 1994). A second generation of cultural difference theorists who are concerned about the disparities in academic achievement between mainstream students and students who are marginalized within the schools and the larger society have done research and constructed theories that have generated teaching implications for the cultural difference paradigm. These scholars include Kathryn H. Au (1993), Gloria Ladson-Billings (1994), Lisa Delpit (1995), Jacqueline Jordan Irvine (2003), Luis Moll (Moll & González, 2004), and Sonia Nieto (2010). These scholars have constructed a theory of culturally responsive teaching (also called culturally sensitive pedagogy) that gives hope and guidance to educators who are trying to improve the academic achievement of students from diverse racial, ethnic, cultural, linguistic, and social-class groups. This theory postulates that the discontinuities between the school culture and the home and community cultures of low-income students and students of color are an important factor in their low academic achievement. Consequently, the academic achievement of these students will increase if schools and teachers reflect and draw on their cultural and linguistic strengths.

Since the publication of her seminal and widely cited article on participation structures in a reading lesson with Hawaiian children in *Anthropology and Education Quarterly* in 1980, Kathryn Au has been one of the most respected, influential, and eloquent voices for culturally responsive teaching and the cultural rights of marginalized and language minority students. The strong empirical base that underlies her arguments and conclusions is one of the hallmarks and distinctive characteristics of her significant work. The intricate and complex ways in which her writing and theories are embedded within and reflect practice further distinguish her theory, research, and recommendations for school reform.

Kathryn Au has spent 25 years as a reflective school practitioner in classrooms with Native Hawaiian children. In this engaging and informative collection of her writing, Au's perceptive cultural eye, keen and power-

ful insights, research rigor, and commitment to social justice are evident
on every page. Au explicates her constructivist conception of culturally
responsive teaching, responds thoughtfully and clearly to questions that
teachers frequently ask about culturally responsive teaching, and uses
empirical data to argue convincingly that "a sure and steady fix, not a quick
one" is essential to reform schools in ways that will help close the achievement gap and provide cultural recognition and equality for students from
diverse groups.

This engaging, heartfelt, and theoretically rich book will help practicing educators deal effectively with the growing ethnic, cultural, and linguistic diversity within U. S. society and schools. American classrooms are
experiencing the largest influx of immigrant students since the beginning
of the 20th century. Nearly one million immigrants are making the United
States their home each year (Martin & Midgley, 2006). Between 1997 and
2006, more than 9 million immigrants entered the United States (U. S.
Department of Homeland Security, 2007). Only 15% came from nations in
Europe. Most came from nations in Asia, from Mexico, and from nations
in Latin America, Central America, and the Caribbean (U. S. Department
of Homeland Security, 2007). A large but undetermined number of undoc-
umented immigrants also enter the United States each year. In 2007, *The
New York Times* estimated that 12 million illegal immigrants were living
in the United States (Immigration Sabotage, 2007). The influence of an
increasingly ethnically diverse population on U. S. schools, colleges, and
universities is, and will continue to be, enormous.

Schools in the United States are more diverse today than they have
been at any point since the early 1900s, when a multitude of immigrants
entered the United States from Southern, Central, and Eastern Europe. In
the 34-year period between 1973 and 2007, the percentage of students of
color in U. S. public schools increased from 22 to 42.3 percent (Dillon,
2006; National Center for Education Statistics, 2008a). If current trends
continue, students of color will equal or exceed the percentage of White
students in U. S. public schools within one or two decades. In the 2007–
2008 school year, students of color exceeded the number of White students
in 11 states: Arizona, California, Florida, Georgia, Hawai'i, Louisiana,
Maryland, Mississippi, New Mexico, Nevada, and Texas (National Center
for Education Statistics, 2008a, 2008b).

Language and religious diversity is also increasing in the U. S. student population. In 2000, about 20% of the school-age population spoke

a language at home other than English (U. S. Census Bureau, 2003). The Progressive Policy Institute estimated that 50 million Americans (out of 300 million) spoke a language at home other than English in 2008. Harvard professor Diana L. Eck (2001) calls the United States the "most religiously diverse nation on Earth" (p. 4). Islam is now the fastest-growing religion in the United States and in several European nations such as France, the United Kingdom, and the Netherlands (Banks, 2009; Cesari, 2004). Most teachers now in the classroom and in teacher education programs will have students from diverse ethnic, racial, linguistic, and religious groups in their classrooms. This is true for both inner-city and suburban teachers in the United States as well as in many other Western nations (Banks, 2009).

The major purpose of the Multicultural Education Series is to provide preservice educators, practicing educators, graduate students, scholars, and policy makers with an interrelated and comprehensive set of books that summarizes and analyzes important research, theory, and practice related to the education of ethnic, racial, cultural, and linguistic groups in the United States and the education of mainstream students about diversity. The dimensions of multicultural education, developed by Banks (2004) and described in the *Handbook of Research on Multicultural Education*, provide the conceptual framework for the development of the publications in the Series. They are: content integration, the knowledge construction process, prejudice reduction, an equity pedagogy, and an empowering institutional culture and social structure.

The books in the Series provide research, theoretical, and practical knowledge about the behaviors and learning characteristics of students of color, language minority students, and low-income students. They also provide knowledge about ways to improve academic achievement and race relations in educational settings. Multicultural education is consequently as important for middle-class White suburban students as it is for inner-city students of color. Multicultural education fosters the public good and the overarching goals of the commonwealth.

Au enriches this gracefully written and incisive book with stories about her family and her account of growing up Chinese American in Hawai'i. She makes a compelling case for schools to respect and honor the languages and cultures of students from diverse groups by poignantly describing the loss of her family language. Au illustrates how schools can create learning communities in which students can be academically successful and acquire ownership of their learning while still maintaining their cultures, identities, and languages. A unique contribution of this informative and practical book is Au's description of how transformative literacy teaching can help students to read both the word and the world (Freire, 1970) and to act to change the world to make it more just and humane. Teachers, principals, researchers, and policy makers will not only be intellectually enriched by reading this timely book, they will also acquire practical and empirically verified knowledge about ways to initiate school reform that will make schools more effective, compassionate, and joyous places.

REFERENCES

Au, K. (1980). Participation structures in a reading lesson with Hawaiian children: Analysis of a culturally appropriate instructional event. *Anthropology and Education Quarterly, 11*(2), 91–115.

Au, K. (1993). *Literacy instruction in multicultural settings.* New York: Harcourt Brace Jovanovich.

Banks, J. A. (2004). Multicultural education: Historical development, dimensions, and practice. In J. A. Banks & C. A. M. Banks (Eds.). *Handbook of research on multicultural education* (2nd ed., pp. 3–29). San Francisco: Jossey-Bass.

Banks, J. A. (Ed.). (2009). *The Routledge international companion to multicultural education.* New York and London: Routledge.

Banks, J. A. & Banks, C. A. M. (Eds.) (2004). *Handbook of research on multicultural education* (2nd ed.). San Francisco: Jossey-Bass.

Bloom, B. S., Davis, A., & Hess, R. (1965). *Compensatory education for cultural deprivation.* New York: Holt.

Boykin, A. W. (1986). The triple quandary and the schooling of Afro-American children. In U. Neisser (Ed.), *The school achievement of minority children: New perspectives* (pp. 57–92). Hillside, NJ: Erlbaum.

Cesari, J. (2004). *When Islam and democracy meet: Muslims in Europe and the United States.* New York: Pelgrave Macmillan.

Delpit, L. (1995). *Other people's children: Cultural conflict in the classroom.* New York: The New Press.

Dillon, S. (2006, August 27). In schools across U. S., the melting pot overflows. *The New York Times*, vol. CLV [155] (no. 53,684), pp. A7 & 16.

Eck, D. L. (2001). *A new religious America: How a "Christian country" has become the world's most religiously diverse nation.* New York: HarperSanFrancisco.

Edmonds, R. (1986). Characteristics of effective schools. In U. Neisser (Ed.), *The school achievement of minority children: New perspectives* (pp. 93-104). Hillside, NJ: Erlbaum.

Freire, P. (1970). *Pedagogy of the oppressed.* New York: Continuum.

Green, R. L. (Ed.). (2009). *Expectations in education: Readings on high expectations, effective teaching, and student engagement.* Columbus, OH: McGraw-Hill/SRA.

Harrington, M. (1962). *The other America: Poverty in the United States.* New York: Macmillan.

Irvine, J. J. (2003). *Educating teachers for diversity: Seeing with a cultural eye.* New York: Teachers College Press.

Immigration sabotage [Editorial]. (2007, June 4). *New York Times,* p. A22.

Ladson-Billings, G. (1994). *The dreamkeepers: Successful teachers of African American children.* San Francisco: Jossey-Bass.

Lee, C. D. (2007). *Culture, literacy, and learning: Taking bloom in the midst of the whirlwind.* New York: Teachers College Press.

Martin, P. & Midgley, E. (1999). Immigration to the United States. *Population Bulletin, 54*(2), pp. 1–44. Washington, D.C.: Population Reference Bureau.

Moll, L. & González, N. (2004). Engaging life: A funds-of-knowledge approach to multicultural education. In J. A. Banks & C. A. M. Banks (Eds.), *Handbook of research on multicultural education* (2nd ed., pp. 699–715). San Francisco: Jossey-Bass.

National Center for Education Statistics (2008a). *The condition of education 2008.* Washington, DC: U. S. Department of Education. Retrieved August 26, 2009, from http://nces.ed.gov/pubsearch/pubsinfo.asp?pubid=2008031

National Center for Education Statistics (2008b). *Public elementary/secondary school universe survey, 2007–2008. Common Core of Data.* Retrieved January, 20, 2010, from http://nces.ed.gov/ccd

National Center for Education Statistics. (2008c). *State nonfiscal survey of public elementary/secondary education, 2007-2008. Common Core of Data.* Retrieved January, 20, 2010, from http://nces.ed.gov/ccd

Nieto, S. (2010). *The light in their eyes: Creating multicultural learning communities* (10th anniversary ed). New York: Teachers College Press.

Progressive Policy Institute. (2008). *50 million Americans speak languages other than English at home.* Retrieved September 2, 2008, from www.ppionline.org/ppi_ci.cf m?knlgAreaID=108&subsecID=900003&contentID=254619

Ramírez, M., & Castañeda, A. (1974). *Cultural democracy, bicognitive development, and education.* New York: Academic Press.

Roberts, S. (2008, August 14). A generation away, minorities may become the majority in U. S. *The New York Times,* vol. CLVII [175] (no. 54,402), pp. A1 & A18.

Ryan, W. (1971). *Blaming the victim.* New York: Pantheon.

U. S. Census Bureau (2003, October). *Language use and English-speaking ability: 2000.* Retrieved September 2, 2008, from www.census.gov/prod/2003pubs/c2kbr-29.pdf

U.S. Census Bureau (2008, August 14). *Statistical abstract of the United States.* Retrieved August 20, 2008 from www.census.gov/prod/2006pubs/07statab/pop.pdf

United States Department of Homeland Security (2007). *Yearbook of immigration statistics, 2006.* Washington, DC: Office of Immigration Statistics, Author. Retrieved August 11, 2009, from www.dhs.gov/files/statistics/publications/yearbook.shtm

Wang, M. C. & Gordon, E. W. (Eds.). (1994). *Educational resilience in inner-city America: Challenges and prospects.* Hillside, NJ: Erlbaum.

Foreword

Even though my schedule didn't warrant an additional task, I gladly accepted the opportunity to write the foreword for this book. When I read the manuscript, I wholeheartedly wanted to endorse Kathryn Au's work. Writing the foreword became quite personal, and I began to reminisce about growing up in the Deep South during the 1950s, 1960s, and early 1970s. I was a member of the second group of Black students to attend the previously all-White Albany High School. It was the late 1960s when the multicultural education movement emerged, and it grew energetically during the 1970s. Three forces converged during the mid-1960s to support this movement: (1) The Civil Rights Movement matured; (2) school textbooks were being critically analyzed; and (3) assumptions underlying deficit views of diverse learners were reassessed (Gay, 1983).

Members of the Civil Rights Movement severely criticized schools for perpetuating the deficiency orientation through institutional processes and teacher classroom practices, not to mention teacher preparation programs. It became apparent that many teachers knew little about students of color and treated *cultural differences* (e.g., differences in speech patterns, language, and ways of interacting socially) as *deficiencies* needing remediation. As Gay (1983) indicates, "[this] new thinking about cultural differences provided the stimulus for the multiethnic education programs" (p. 561).

Multiculturalism in education became a *concept* that most teacher educators professed to understand a great deal—even if they knew little or nothing about it—because policy mandates required the inclusion of multicultural content in their courses (Sleeter & Grant, 1994). Although the incongruence between preservice teachers' cultural insularity and children's pluralism became more recognized, relatively little attention was paid in teacher education programs on preparing teachers for pluralistic classrooms (Grant & Secada, 1990; Liston & Zeichner, 1991, Sleeter, 1985).

James Banks (1995) argued that "if multicultural education is to become better understood and implemented in ways more consistent with theory, its various dimensions must be more clearly described, conceptualized, and researched" (pp. 3–4). In response, teacher educators began to pose questions such as, "What do teacher candidates need to become effective teachers?" and "What do teacher candidates need to become effective multicultural teachers in our pluralistic society?" (Chisholm, 1994, p. 43).

These kinds of questions shifted discussions on multicultural education from a *concept* to a *commitment* (see Lazar, 2004; Tatum, 2005), leading educators to understand the importance of acknowledging and integrating students' cultural backgrounds in the teaching and learning process. Kathyrn Au's work moved educators to this new reality. Moreover, what emerged from her research over the years were the keys to success in the teaching and learning of literacy with culturally and linguistically diverse students.

With a shift in thinking toward a *commitment* to multicultural education, cultural relevance and responsiveness as pedagogical and instructional concepts gained increasing attention among teacher educators and literacy researchers. *Culturally relevant teaching,* identified as an instructional approach that promotes academic success with culturally and linguistically diverse students, is grounded in theories of cultural compatibility (Jordan, 1985; Vogt, Jordan, & Tharp, 1987), cultural appropriateness (Au, 1980), and cultural responsiveness (Erickson & Mohatt, 1982; Gay, 2000; Hollins, 1996). Culturally relevant pedagogies represent the highest levels of accommodation of student diversity through culturally mediated instruction. Defined also as "a pedagogy that empowers students intellectually, socially, emotionally, and politically by using cultural referents to impart knowledge, skills, and attitudes" (Ladson-Billings, 1994, p. 18), it not only uses "student culture" as a means for bridging or explaining the dominant culture, but it also places students' cultural knowledge, practices, and experiences at the center of curriculum and instruction. A research synthesis of the literature suggests that providing literacy instruction that is culturally relevant and responsive promotes high achievement among culturally and linguistically diverse students (Gay, 2000; Hale, 2001; Ladson-Billings, 1994; Nichols, Rupley, & Webb-Johnson, 2000).

Kathryn Au continues to lead teacher educators and researchers in addressing culturally relevant pedagogies. As Au crafted her insightful, thoughtful, and research-based manuscripts, practitioners, teacher educators, and literacy researchers waited with anticipation. *Literacy Achievement and Diversity* presents Au's most widely cited ideas. This book is designed to help teachers, administrators, teacher educators, and literacy researchers engage in a comprehensive discussion about culturally and linguistically diverse students.

However, it is important to point out that this is not a recipe book. This book motivates the reader to think critically about culturally and linguistically diverse students. After completing this "must-read" book, you will gain new understandings about yourself, about others, and about culturally relevant pedagogies. You will see that it is indeed possible to close the literacy achievement gap.

—Patricia A. Edwards
East Lansing, Michigan

Acknowledgments

Many thanks are due to Taffy Raphael, who was the first reader of most of the material contained in this book. Thanks are also due to Barbara Taylor, who gave so generously of her time and expertise to conduct the hierarchical linear modeling analysis presented in Chapter 7.

Introduction

What can educators do to improve the literacy learning of students of diverse cultural and linguistic backgrounds? This is the question that has guided my research and intellectual journey for over 30 years. My purpose in this book is to share my understandings about the theoretical framing of the issues, the results of my research and the research of others, and recommended solutions for educators working in schools. The overall message of this book is that it *can* be done—the literacy achievement gap can be closed, and culturally responsive instruction is an important part of the solution. We can bring students of diverse backgrounds to high levels of literacy, in classrooms where learning can be joyful, and in schools where educators have a strong sense of community and purpose.

This book has been designed for possible use in graduate courses on literacy and diversity and in teacher study groups. It will be suitable for use in both university courses and school settings because its content covers theory, research, and practice. It should appeal to researchers and practitioners who are interested in improving not only the literacy achievement of students of diverse backgrounds, but also academic achievement in general, since literacy is widely understood to underlie learning in many areas. It should also be of interest to teacher educators who teach language arts methods courses for preservice or inservice teachers, as well as courses on multicultural education and multicultural issues in literacy.

How can this vision of bringing all students to high levels of literacy be made a reality? This book highlights four Keys to Success that have emerged from my research over the years. Key to Success #1 is understanding that the challenge is complexly determined and multifaceted, and therefore the response to the challenge must be multifaceted, as well. I argue that educators must orient themselves toward the sure and steady fix, rather than yielding to the temptation of the quick fix, which only leads to a fruitless search for the nonexistent "perfect program."

While the challenge of improving literacy achievement in classrooms and schools with many students of diverse backgrounds is complex and requires thoughtful analysis, there is considerable knowledge about how this challenge can be met. The factors to be considered can be identified (e.g., higher-level thinking with text, culturally responsive instruction, assessment that guides instruction, and positive relationships with parents and the community), and there is research to suggest how these factors come together to provide a comprehensive solution at the level of classrooms and schools. At the same time, we must constantly be aware of the power relations and historical forces, including assimilationist ideology, working against efforts to close the achievement gap.

Key to Success #2 in improving the literacy achievement of students of diverse cultural and linguistic backgrounds is providing ample instruction focused on higher-level thinking with text, or reading comprehension. An emphasis on high-interest texts, along with personally meaningful literacy activities, helps to promote students' ownership of literacy. Accountability pressures tend to fall hardest on schools enrolling many students of diverse backgrounds, especially in urban and rural communities with a history of low test scores. A common response to accountability pressures has been an intensification of testing and a rush to quick-fix programs that overemphasize lower-level skills and underemphasize student ownership of literacy and authentic purposes. In this book I explain why this response is misguided and what alternative courses of action can and should be pursued.

Key to Success #3 in improving literacy achievement is building upon the strengths that students of diverse cultural and linguistic backgrounds bring from the home. This, of course, is the idea behind culturally responsive instruction. Culturally responsive instruction has been an appealing concept, but a sound understanding of this concept and its practical implications has not yet gained traction among educators. I develop several lines of argument. One is that culturally responsive instruction is a concept that applies to all students, including those of mainstream backgrounds, not just to students of diverse backgrounds. Another is that culturally responsive instruction has to do with building on values reflected in a diverse worldview, with the practical implication that teachers must be aware of incorporating a variety of participation structures or interactional patterns throughout the school day. I also describe how constructivist approaches—specifically, the writers' workshop and the process approach to writing, and the readers' workshop and literature-based instruction—provide this variety of participation structures.

Key to Success #4 in improving the literacy achievement of students of diverse backgrounds is developing schoolwide professional learning communities where teachers can pull together to accomplish a shared vision of excellence in literacy achievement for their students. Ultimately, it is teachers—not programs—that make the difference by changing the nature of teaching and learning interactions in classrooms. Students of diverse cultural and linguistic backgrounds often enter the classroom with literacy achievement below grade level standards, primarily due to a lack of opportunity to develop literacy knowledge and strategies valued in school. It is not enough for a school to have well-prepared, conscientious teachers who understand the nature of effective instruction, if those teachers are working independently with little knowledge of one another's efforts. Instead of working in isolation, teachers must collaborate as a schoolwide professional learning community to build a coherent or staircase curriculum in literacy so that their students will have consistent instruction across the grades.

In short, my goal in this book is to provide educators with a solid grounding in the theoretical and research foundations for building on students' strengths as an overall strategy for improving literacy achievement, centering on the four Keys to Success. My intention is to give the reader a sense of the major issues that must be addressed in efforts to close the literacy achievement gap, especially from the perspective of the school and classroom. These major issues, which parallel the four Keys to Success, include:

1. An overall theory of why the literacy achievement gap exists and how it can be overcome.
2. How to provide effective instruction of phonics and basic skills while maintaining the focus on meaning necessary for students' later success as readers and writers.
3. Why culturally responsive instruction should be part of every teacher's repertoire and specific ideas for implementing culturally responsive instruction.
4. An approach to whole-school change that extends constructivist principles of learning by providing a framework in which teachers create their school's own staircase or coherent curriculum in literacy.

Each chapter examines two or more of the four Keys to Success. Chapters are introduced with a brief set of comments explaining the Keys to Success emphasized and the important points I hope readers will grasp. I provide guidance about research and practical issues and suggest follow-up activities that readers may wish to pursue.

This volume also includes a narrative thread, describing the family and professional experiences and values that shaped my work and the evolution of my thinking over the course of my academic career. Chapter 1 is an intellectual autobiography, while Chapters 3, 4, and 7 also incorporate family history and personal experience.

Because the literacy achievement gap reflects the inequalities in society as a whole, including the widening chasm between the rich and the poor, some critics take issue with reform-minded approaches. They insist that there is little educators can do to make a difference given societal conditions. My attitude is quite the opposite. As I show in this volume, we have detailed knowledge of how to close the literacy achievement gap. Having spent my career working in schools in high-poverty communities, I know firsthand the challenges faced by educators in these settings. Yet I have seen determined principals, teachers, students, families, and communities pull together to make substantial improvements in students' literacy learning. We can close the literacy achievement gap by applying the four Keys to Success, and now is the time to do so.

Chapter 1

Schooling, Literacy, and Cultural Diversity in Research and Personal Experience

My research stance has been characterized as that of a reformer, which is an accurate description of my intentions. I hope my research will contribute to the improvement of literacy instruction in classrooms with students of diverse cultural backgrounds.

The question of how to close the literacy achievement gap has been much debated among researchers, and many different analyses of the problem, as well as a wide variety of solutions, have been proposed. Because of the wealth of information available, I believe that readers should understand the positionality of the researcher whose ideas are being considered. It is in this light that I discuss the evolution of my interest in the literacy achievement gap and culturally responsive instruction, which began with my personal experience growing up as a Chinese American in Hawai'i. These experiences shaped my beliefs about schooling, literacy, and cultural diversity.

This chapter traces my development as an educator and educational researcher through the early years of my career, up to my initial research on talk-story-like participation structures and culturally responsive instruction. I spent my first two decades as an educator at the Kamehameha Elementary Education Program (KEEP), a project focused on closing the literacy achievement gap for students of Native Hawaiian ancestry. The issues affecting the literacy achievement of Native Hawaiian students parallel those affecting the literacy achievement of many other students of diverse cultural and linguistic backgrounds in the United States and around the world. The literacy achievement gap is a systemic issue. As indicated in Key to Success #1, the gap is complexly determined, and we must understand existing patterns that serve to perpetuate it. Then we must work to

put in place new patterns that will significantly improve students' opportunities to achieve high levels of literacy. Work conducted at KEEP highlights
the importance of Key to Success #2, an emphasis on higher-level thinking
with text, or reading comprehension, as a new pattern critical in promoting students' literacy learning.

Of the studies I have conducted, those on talk-story-like reading lessons are the most cited. These studies align with Key to Success #3, building on the strengths students bring from the home through culturally
responsive instruction. In these studies I showed that teachers effective
in teaching reading to young Native Hawaiian students did not conduct
discussion following the pattern for classroom recitation observed in
mainstream classrooms (Au, 1980). Rather, they conducted discussions
following rules similar to those for a *talk story*, a Hawaiian community
speech event. During talk story, participants speak in rhythmic alterna-
tion with a high degree of overlapping speech as they share in the retelling
of events. When Hawaiian students participated in talk-story-like lessons,
as opposed to mainstream recitation lessons, they showed higher rates
of academic behaviors related to learning to read: They spent more time
focused on the reading task, discussed more story ideas, and made more
logical inferences about the story (Au & Mason, 1981). These studies were
among the first to verify the possibility of improving the academic learning
of students of diverse backgrounds through the use of culturally responsive
instruction, that is, instruction reflecting values and practices similar to
those of the home culture. These studies, and others that I have conducted,
highlight the themes of schooling, literacy, and cultural diversity.

SCHOOLING AND FAMILY HISTORY

I cannot remember a time when I did not think of schooling as a precious
commodity, so family members must have instilled this notion in me at an
early age. Although I did not always like going to school, I never doubted
the goodness of the abstract idea of school. Because I grew up believing
that education would be the key to my own success in life, it was easy for
me to come to believe as a professional that education would be the key to
helping students of diverse backgrounds achieve a better life.

I am a Chinese American and in the fourth generation of my family
to live in Hawai'i. I have always had an interest in family history, particu-

larly in the lives of my grandmothers, and have been consciously gathering information about my family's past for many years. My maternal grandmother died in 1985 at the age of 103, and my paternal grandmother died in 1998 at the age of 100. In their last years, while forgetful of recent events, both my grandmothers had clear memories of the distant past.

Grandmother Hew

Many generations of men in my family have had the chance to attend school and to learn to read and write. However, only in the past two or three generations have women had this opportunity. My maternal grandmother, Hew Ngim Moi, could not read or write in either Chinese or English, a fact she regretted all her life. Grandmother Hew was born in the Hakka village of Nam Wai, in the New Territories near Hong Kong, in 1883. Her father, Shinn Sam Shing, left for Hawai'i that same year. As the third son in a poor village family, he went in search of a brighter future. He worked as a bookkeeper for a Chinese merchant and also earned money by writing letters for his acquaintances who wished to communicate with their families back in China. Thirteen years passed before he was able to send for his wife and daughter.

While growing up in the village, Grandmother Hew did not go to school because only boys could attend. But she wanted to go to school and was very curious about what went on there. One day she climbed a tree so she could get a better look. Throughout my career that image of my grandmother as a young girl, on the outside looking in, has inspired me to try to make a high-quality education accessible to more students.

When Grandmother Hew came to Hawai'i, she and her parents lived in Kula on the island of Maui. Quite a few Chinese families lived in the area at the time, most earning their living as farmers. My grandmother lived with her parents in a shed originally built to store corn. She walked across the hilly countryside to gather firewood for cooking and to draw water from a stream. She and her mother found life more difficult than in the village, where they had been surrounded by family and the work could be shared. Although the neighbors in Kula were generous, they were not close at hand.

In theory, Grandmother Hew could have attended the public school in Kula. However, her parents, like others of their generation, believed that education was important for boys but not for girls; since a Chinese woman became part of her husband's family after she married, her parents' investment in her education was considered to be wasted. Also, my grandmother's help was needed to run the household and the farm and, later, to care for the younger children. I once asked my grandmother whether there were truant officers who could have required her parents to send her to school. She laughed. When the truant officers came around, she said, the families simply hid the girls. At any rate, by the time she had been in Kula a few years, she was considered too old to go to school.

Although Grandmother Hew never had the chance to go to school, she supported the education of her brothers and sister. Grandmother Hew's four younger siblings were all born in Kula. They attended public school, and after that school let out for the day, they went to classes at the community-sponsored Chinese school. Her first brother, Tenn Sung Shinn, attended St. Anthony, a Catholic high school, where he could study business. While at St. Anthony, Tenn Sung lived at the home of my grandmother, who was now married. He worked at a store after school and gave my grandmother everything he earned in return for his room and board. Although she had a growing family of her own, my grandmother never spent any of his money. When he graduated, she returned the full amount to him, and he in turn gave the money to his parents.

Mun Fook Shinn, Grandmother Hew's second brother, attended St. Anthony for a year but then contracted tuberculosis and went to the Kula sanitarium where he learned to be a laboratory technician. According to Great-Uncle Mun Fook, the expectations for education changed rapidly among the Chinese families in Kula in the early 1900s. Men his age thought themselves lucky to continue past the eighth grade, but those only a few years younger were among the first to graduate from college. As the educational expectations for boys rose, the families also began to send girls to school, and this practice had become common by about 1905.

Mabel Shinn Liu, my grandmother's sister, benefited from the changing views of women's education. She completed grade school in Kula and then spent a year at Maunaolu Seminary, a girls' high school. Her education came to an end when she too contracted tuberculosis. Barring illness, she might have become a teacher like the other Chinese women who attended Maunaolu.

When my great-grandparents returned to China in 1922, my grandmother's youngest brother, Chyau On Shinn, went with them. During several sojourns to Hawai'i during the 1930s and 1940s, he imported Chinese goods and ran a grocery store with Mabel's help.

Grandmother Hew married at the age of 19, and my mother is the youngest of her eight children. Following the customs of the time, she did not see her new husband, Hew Sing Cha, until the day of the wedding. My grandfather became a cook and baker serving the Chinese laborers on the sugar plantation in Pā'ia. Later, the family ran a store and restaurant in Pā'ia. They spoke Chinese at home, and my mother (and probably her brothers and sisters as well) did not speak any English before entering school. Grandmother Hew walked her children to and from school and took a great interest in their education.

My oldest uncle, Chong Meo Hew, graduated from St. Anthony and then went to work, making it possible for his seven younger brothers and sisters to continue their education. In his generation, he took the role my grandmother had taken in hers, of caring for and supporting the younger children. All graduated from Maui High School, and all but one went on to higher education. Poor health prevented Richard, the youngest son, from moving to O'ahu to attend the university.

Grandmother Hew wanted her daughters, as well as her sons, to be well educated. My mother, aunts, and uncles all speak of this fact with pride. In the 1920s and 1930s my grandmother's views about the education of women ran counter to those of most members of Pā'ia's Chinese community. One day my grandmother got into a heated argument with a Mr. Wong. He contended that girls should not go on to higher education, that they should just be married off. Mr. Wong's remarks upset my grandmother. Eventually, one of my aunts, Ah Kewn, called him a troublemaker and chased him out of the house. The story of my grandmother's argument with the peanut man (Mr. Wong earned his living by selling boiled peanuts) is part of the lore of our family, and over the years I have heard it repeated many times.

As Grandmother Hew hoped, my mother and her three sisters all went on to higher education. Two of my mother's sisters had careers that in some ways prefigured my own. My first aunt, Ah Lun Hew Zane, went to the Territorial Normal School and later received a bachelor's degree in education from the University of Hawai'i. She taught first on Maui, then on O'ahu. My second aunt, Ah Kewn Hew, received a certificate (the equivalent of a master's degree today) from the New York School of Social Work in 1940, an unusual achievement at the time. When she returned to Maui, she was one of only two social workers on the island.

Until I was a teenager, I spent all of my summer vacations at the house in Pā'ia. After dinner, Grandmother Hew and the adult relatives often "talked story," reminiscing and gossiping in a mixture of Hakka and English. My grandmother was a skillful storyteller with an excellent memory, and others in the circle often turned to her with questions. As a child I did not participate in these discussions, but I developed an appreciation for uses of language and literacy that did not necessarily involve English or a printed text.

Grandmother Hew had a lively intelligence and quick wit and took an active interest in everything around her. Sometimes she and I would sit on the sofa downstairs and look at photographs in the pages of *Life, Look* and other magazines. She always spoke to me in English, and I did not learn to speak Hakka, although I could understand a few common phrases. I do not recall when I became aware that my grandmother could not read. I know that by the time I was about 8 or 9, I was reading captions to her or scanning the text so I could answer her questions about the photographs.

When I was an adult and thought to question my grandmother about her literacy, I learned that she could read a calendar and prices and recognize a few words in English and in Chinese. If she saw the words often enough, she said, after a while she could figure out what they were. I discovered that she had learned some Hawaiian, Ilokano, and Japanese through working in the store and other contacts with people in the community. Late in life, she learned to sign her name in English.

Grandmother Au

My paternal grandmother, Katherine Choy Kan Ahana Au, was born in Hawai'i on the island of Kaua'i in 1898. She was the sixth of the twelve children of Chun Lin Hung and Jay Shee. His Chinese acquaintances called my great-grandfather Ah Hung, a name the Hawaiians pronounced as Ahana, and for this reason Ahana replaced Chun as the family surname. My grandmother and her siblings grew up in Hulēi'a, where my great-grandfather had a rice mill and plantation.

When she was 9 or 10 years old, Grandmother Au began to attend the one-room school in Hulēi'a. Her brothers and sisters had already taught her to read and write in English, and when she got to school, she discovered that the teacher knew less than some of his pupils. One day, she and a couple of other students gave their teacher a little test. They wrote out the word *bouquet* and asked him to pronounce it. As they had predicted, he told them the word was "bo-ket."

Around the age of 12, Grandmother Au began to attend Līhu'e School, taking a horse-drawn cart to town and back every day. She liked to study and was eager to learn, and she and a Japanese boy became the best students in their class. She did not think that most of the teachers knew how to help the students learn. The exception was a Mrs. Burke, who went step-by-step through the lessons so that everyone understood, instead of rushing through as the other teachers did.

Grandmother Au wanted to continue past the eighth grade, but her father did not think his daughters should get any more education than that. At the time, my grandmother said, a girl considered herself lucky to be able to go even that far in school. Still, my grandmother was disappointed because she loved school. When she told her teacher that she would be quitting, her teacher was shocked. "What?" she said. "With your grades?"

Even before Grandmother Au had completed the eighth grade, Miss Huntley, the supervising principal, asked her to serve as a substitute teacher at Līhu'e School. My grandmother would go to class for a while, but then when a teacher was absent, she would have to act as a substitute until the teacher returned. She felt honored and cheated at the same time.

Grandmother Au worked as a substitute teacher off and on until she was married. Her duties as a substitute teacher varied. One year, she had to enroll 102 first-year students. She pinned notes to their backs asking their parents to supply birth dates and other necessary information, and she completed the paperwork so that everything was in order by the time the regular teacher arrived. Her sister-in-law, Dora Peiler Ahana, became the teacher at Hulēi'a School, and when Dora's parents died, Grandmother Au had to take over. She learned of her new responsibilities through instructions shouted to her from the road. With no warning and no books or other materials, she assumed Dora's duties. She worried about not knowing what to do, but she managed until Dora's return.

Following the customs of the day, my paternal great-grandparents stressed the education of the boys but not the girls. My grandmother's two older brothers were sent to private schools in Honolulu; Koon Chong graduated from 'Iolani and Koon Ming from St. Louis. My grandmother's two younger brothers graduated from Kaua'i High School. Of her six sisters, only the youngest, Harriet, graduated from high school.

Until she was in her early nineties and her eyesight became poor, Grandmother Au was an avid letter writer. She corresponded with dozens of people and for years mailed out more than 300 cards at Christmas. A member of the Līhu'e Baptist Church since 1937, she was active in church activities, especially after her sons were grown. Because of her strong religious beliefs, she read the Bible nearly every day. She read many books and pamphlets with religious themes, and I do not recall seeing her read any secular material apart from popular women's magazines, such as *Ladies' Home Journal.*

My family, like other Chinese American families in Hawai'i, experienced dramatic increases in levels of education both within and between generations. The education of men and women did not follow the same pattern, in part because of beliefs brought from China about the education of women. One of my grandmothers did not have a chance to go to school at all, and the other did not go as far in school as she wished. Both treasured literacy, one because she could not read and write, the other because she found it to be of great social and religious value. As a child I did not know of my grandmothers' specific experiences with schooling, only of the value they placed on education. Later, when I knew to ask, I found that their feelings of disappointment about their own schooling had not been dimmed by the years or by the successes of their children.

In my parents' generation, education for women became the norm. Interestingly, in my mother's family it was an aunt, not an uncle, who received a graduate degree. This, I believe, was due to Grandmother Hew's influence. Because my mother and aunts were well educated, I grew up with high expectations for my own schooling. But access to higher levels of schooling, particularly for women, was new enough in the history of my family that I did not take education for granted.

CULTURE AND LANGUAGE

My interest in research on culturally responsive instruction derives in part from my own experiences as a Chinese American. I do not hyphenate the term *Chinese American* because I agree with the argument that a hyphen between *Chinese* and *American* suggests that the two can be broken apart. Rather, I prefer the view that Chinese defines a kind of American (W. Lum, 1990). Every American is some kind of American, and I feel that issues of cultural identity should be explored by all students, not just by students of diverse backgrounds. However, for students of diverse backgrounds, it may be more difficult to find a balance between assimilating to mainstream culture and maintaining a commitment to their own cultural heritage.

My parents, like other Asian Americans of their generation in Hawai'i, were deeply influenced by the events of World War II. A photograph of my mother, Mun Kyau Hew Au, receiving her high school diploma, shows her with a gas mask draped across one shoulder; Pearl Harbor had been bombed the previous December. Nevertheless, my mother moved to Honolulu from Maui to attend the University of Hawai'i, where she received her training in laboratory science and medical technology. She spent her senior year working in the lab at Queen's Hospital in Honolulu and graduated with a bachelor of science degree in chemistry and biology.

My father, Harold Kwock Ung Au, moved to Honolulu from Kaua'i to live with relatives so he could attend the university. On the morning of December 7, 1941, he and his cousin saw planes pass overhead as they were on their way to play tennis. Assuming the planes to be American, they continued on to the courts. When they returned home, they learned of the bombing of Pearl Harbor. My father was already a member of the Varsity Volunteers, a unit of university students. Along with other Asian students determined to prove their loyalty to the United States, he quit school to serve full time in the Territorial Guard.

The war and its aftermath probably accelerated the process of assimilation of Chinese American families in Hawai'i, although this process was already well under way. When I was growing up, we observed Chinese customs, such as the ceremonies of the New Year and the memorial season, and we acquired a sense of family values. However, we lost the use of Chinese as the language of everyday communication. My parents both grew up speaking Chinese, but my father's family spoke Cantonese, whereas my mother's family spoke Hakka, a northern language similar to Mandarin. These varieties of Chinese are not mutually intelligible, so my parents' common language was English. But in my friends' families, even when both parents spoke the same dialect, the same situation prevailed: The language spoken in the home was English, not Chinese.

The summer I was 10, my brother, sister, and I attended a Chinese school in downtown Honolulu. The school primarily served families that had recently immigrated, and its program assumed that students could already speak Cantonese but needed to learn to read and write. We felt out of place and quit after 3 weeks. In high school, along with a number of my Chinese American classmates, I studied Mandarin for 2 years. Most of us were there because our parents thought it a good idea, and we did not take our teacher seriously.

As an adult, I realized that I was cut off from part of my past because I could not speak, read, or understand Chinese. I was fortunate that all my grandparents could speak English. But I cannot read for myself the records in the Shinn temple in Man Kung Uk that list the names of my ancestors going back 25 generations. And there are nuances of meaning that I will never understand. After the death of my uncle Richard, I was seated downstairs in the Pā'ia house next to my aunt, Ah Lun, when one of my grandmother's old friends came by to extend her condolences. The woman spoke to my grandmother in Chinese. On hearing her words, my aunt and the others nodded in appreciation. I asked my aunt what the woman had said. My aunt thought for a moment, then told me, "I can't explain it in English. But she said just the right thing."

The process of language loss is swift, can take place in just one generation, and in many cases is irreversible. The case of the Hawaiian language is particularly striking. The Native Hawaiian population at the time of Cook's arrival in 1778 numbered perhaps 400,000. But by the mid-1980s, there were perhaps as few as 30 Hawaiian children being raised to speak their native language. Before the advent of the Hawaiian-language immersion program, initiated in two of Hawai'i's public schools in 1987, the language was in danger of being lost as a means of everyday communication (Wilson, 1991).

Certainly, culture is more than language, but my own experience illustrates a fact verified by recent research with students who come to school speaking a native language other than English. The language of power in the United States is English, a fact well known to these students and their parents, and these students are all learning English. At the same time, they are in danger of losing their native languages (Pease-Alvarez & Hakuta, 1992). Clearly, we need to provide much more support for bilingual education in order to maintain and improve students' command not just of English but of other languages, especially those already spoken by their families. American students, like their counterparts around the world, can and should be literate in at least two languages. Being literate, in this case, would extend to oral as well as written expression, along with knowledge of the cultural concepts and values important to speakers of the language.

LITERACY

In my research I have been interested in the question of how students of diverse backgrounds can become literate through means that do not require them to give up their cultural identities. Literacy can be taught in a manner that either empowers or disempowers (Au & Kaomea, 2009).

The dictionary defines *empower* as "to invest with power, especially legal power or official authority." I think of empowerment somewhat differently, as the confidence to act on one's own behalf. We work toward empowering students through literacy when we help them gain competence in written and oral expression and also understand themselves and their world better through reading, writing, listening, speaking, and observing.

My early experiences with literacy gave me confidence in myself as a learner and a sense of the excitement and power of words. They did not, however, enable me to understand or appreciate my own world and cultural identity.

In the living room of our home on Pacific Heights in Honolulu, my parents assembled a large bookcase from planks and glass blocks, and we children kept our books on the bottom shelf. Most of our books were Little Golden Books, including many of the titles now reissued, such as *The Pokey Little Puppy* (Lowrey, 1942). We had a huge collection because my parents bought us one or two of these books whenever they went out for the evening or took us shopping.

Apparently, my affinity for books developed early. One of my mother's cousins, who came to Hawai'i from Nam Wai as a teenager, remembers her first sight of me. I must have been 3 or 4 years old at the time, and I was sitting on the floor with a pile of books stacked higher than my head. She watched in fascination as I picked up one book after another, going through all of the pages and seemingly reading all the words. At the time she knew no English and so could not understand what I was saying, but this scene was fresh in her mind when she described it to me 30 years later.

My favorite of the Little Golden Books was titled *Little Pond in the Woods* (Ward, 1948). As I recall, it did not have much of a story line, just one animal after another, including a bear, a deer, and a rabbit, coming to the pond to drink. I had heard the story so often that I had memorized it and could recite the text word for word, page by page. Some members of the family were impressed by this feat, but I know that I did not yet understand how to deal with print. When I was in the first grade, my aunt Ah Lun, a teacher, gave me copies of the pre-primers and primer from the Scott, Foresman series. I remember the weekend I suddenly discovered that I could read all the words. I read through all four books. It was an exhilarating experience but it took hours, and at the end I was exhausted.

My parents, aunts, and uncles all read aloud to us. My mother read us nursery rhymes and popular poetry, such as "The Owl and the Pussycat" and Joyce Kilmer's "Trees." We had two books by Dr. Seuss, *Bartholomew and the Oobleck* (1949) and *The 500 Hats of Bartholomew Cubbins* (1938). As we got older, adults read us chapters from *The Wizard of Oz* (Baum, 1903). In addition, we read comic books of all sorts, featuring Donald Duck and Uncle Scrooge, Casper the Friendly Ghost, Archie and his friends, Superman, Batman, and a whole array of other superheroes.

After I had learned to read, my mother bought copies of the books she had enjoyed as a child, so I made the acquaintance of the Bobbsey Twins and the Five Little Peppers. I remember having a book about King Arthur and the knights of the round table. My mother took us to the main branch of the Library of Hawai'i, with its high-ceilinged rooms opening to grassy courtyards. The library was cool, quiet, and orderly, and all the books set neatly on the shelves seemed to be part of their own timeless world. I liked borrowing books from the public library and the library at school. I was overjoyed when I found a new series of books. I read all the Dr. Doolittle books but never discovered Nancy Drew. I liked the books of fairy tales by Andrew Lang and the novels by Louisa May Alcott, Walter Farley, and Laura Ingalls Wilder.

I did not connect reading in school with the rest of the reading I was doing because the two were entirely different. Reading in school, through the sixth grade, meant reading aloud and working one's way through the basal readers, such as *On Cherry Street* (Ousley, 1961). I liked some of the stories in the readers but, beginning in third grade, I had often read them all (surreptitiously) by the second or third week of school. I didn't mind doing workbook exercises, although I know that I didn't learn phonics, including the so-called long and short vowels, until after I could already read. Since I had the same classmates year after year, we developed games such as racing to see who could finish first and still get all the answers right. Mrs. Awai, my fifth-grade teacher, let us go to the library often, and that was the year I read much more than I ever had in school.

The books in the library, as well as our basal readers, presented us with a world quite different from our own. I recall only two books with Asian settings: *The Five Chinese Brothers* (Bishop & Wiese, 1938) and *The Story About Ping* (Flack & Wiese, 1933). Illustrations of the brothers showed them to be horrible caricatures of Asians. Ping, while nicely drawn, was still only a duck. We read books of Hawaiian legends, but none with contemporary Hawaiian characters. As a student, I do not remember thinking it odd never to come across a book written by an Asian American or with Asian American characters or, for that matter, with any but European American characters. I assumed that books were supposed to represent another world, not anything close to my own experience, since that was the case with all the books I had ever read.

In a sense, this disconnectedness between the world depicted in books and my own world paralleled the disconnectedness between school and life outside. I was fortunate to come from a family that valued schooling so much that I never thought to question why schooling should be so divorced from everyday reality. I believe my elementary school teachers, like my parents, leaned toward an assimilationist, rather than pluralist, ideology and were primarily concerned with teaching us what children all over the United States were being taught. In the years following World War II, in fact until the late 1980s, students in Hawai'i's schools did not learn about crucial events in Hawaiian history, particularly the illegal overthrow of the Hawaiian monarchy plotted by American sugar planters.

I am overjoyed that so many wonderful children's books written by authors of diverse backgrounds are now available, and that social studies textbooks are beginning to move away from a Eurocentric bias. Yet I know that many teachers feel uncomfortable teaching literature and social studies from a pluralist versus assimilationist perspective. Many teachers and publishers seem to believe that the reason for introducing children to multicultural literature is to "teach them that people are more alike than different." They do not seem to understand that celebrating and maintaining differences may be equally, if not more, important to students of diverse backgrounds, such as Native Hawaiian students, who sense their cultural identity and heritage being threatened by the larger society.

BECOMING A TEACHER AND RESEARCHER

For the first two decades of my career, I worked at the Kamehameha Elementary Education Program (KEEP). KEEP was an educational change effort that had the goal of improving the literacy achievement of Native Hawaiian students enrolled in schools in low-income communities. The premise of KEEP was that Hawaiian students could achieve at parity with national norms. Until it was closed in 1995, KEEP was the nation's longest-running research and development project devoted to improving the education of students of a particular ethnic group.

I imagine that my choice of research topics might have been quite different had I been based in a university instead of a school. In those years I always tried to focus my research on the key issues facing KEEP. Sometimes the research matched my personal preferences, and sometimes it did not. I liked to conduct small-scale studies, such as those of videotaped small-group reading lessons, in which I had the opportunity to understand features of instruction in depth. I did not particularly like to conduct large-scale studies involving dozens of classrooms and hundreds of students, as in my work on constructivist curricula and portfolio assessment (Au, Scheu, Kawakami, & Herman, 1990; Au, 1994). While my job gave me ample research opportunities and resources, it forced me to become a generalist, exploring a wider range of topics than I feel would have been ideal for a researcher. Usually I did not have the opportunity to tie up the loose ends before I needed to start work on a new issue.

My employment at KEEP came about quite by chance. After a year of courses at the University of Hawai'i, I did my student teaching in a fifth-grade classroom at Wilson School, located in one of Honolulu's middle-class neighborhoods. When I received my professional diploma in June, I felt ready to have a classroom of my own. However, my prospects of finding a job were slim; Hawai'i had far more teachers than it could use. One by one, the women who had completed their student teaching with me went on to other jobs: as a sales clerk in a department store, as a secretary in an insurance firm. I wondered whether my decision to teach had been a good one.

One day my mother noticed a newspaper ad placed by the Kamehameha Schools, a large private school for Native Hawaiian students. They were looking for two teachers to work for a new project. Desirable qualifications included teaching experience, especially with Hawaiian children, and previous work in curriculum development or research. I lacked these qualifications but applied anyway, because I had nothing to lose. I had a brief interview with the director of personnel, then a lengthy interview with the men who would lead the new project, including Ronald Gallimore, a professor in the psychology department at the University of Hawai'i, and Stephen Boggs, an anthropology professor at the same institution. Later, I went to the university for an interview with Roland Tharp, who with Ron was one of the project's principal investigators.

I do not remember the specific content of these interviews, except for learning that research would be a part of the project. I decided it would be best to acknowledge right up front that I did not have the desired experience but that I was willing to learn and to work hard. KEEP's leaders took a chance on me. Their other choice was Arlene Granger, a teacher with many years of experience working with Hawaiian children, and they thought that we would be a good combination.

Arlene and I spent a year learning about curriculum trends in reading throughout the state and visiting public schools enrolling a high percentage of Native Hawaiian students. We observed a wide range of practices and discovered little consensus among educators about the best approach for teaching Hawaiian children to read.

By the fall of 1972, two more teachers, Sherlyn Franklin Goo and Sarah Sueoka, had been hired, and KEEP enrolled its first class of kindergarten students, most of them Native Hawaiians and from families receiving welfare. Our first classroom was the lounge of one of the dormitories on the Kamehameha Schools campus. My fellow teachers had all done much more teaching than I, so they took charge. I started by doing just a few lessons, reading stories to the students and teaching math to a small group using Cuisenaire rods. These children were unlike those I had taught at Wilson, in age as well as socioeconomic and cultural background. I found I had to learn classroom management strategies—quickly.

The enrollment policy at KEEP's laboratory school had been designed to give us the same population of students found in the neighboring public schools, but in fact we ended up with a population including more low-income students than any other school. Even at the age of 5 or 6, the children had developed the skills needed to survive in the public housing projects of Kalihi. They could fight, swear, answer back, and band together. They did not respect me just because I was supposed to be their teacher. I had to earn their respect by showing that I could take charge of the class, respond to challenges, make lessons interesting, and be both kind and tough (for a discussion of classroom management issues with Native Hawaiian students, refer to D'Amato, 1988). In turn, the students showed that they were bright, creative, thoughtful, and loving. I struggled during my first years in the classroom, and I was fortunate in having Arlene, Sarah, and Sherl to serve as models and to advise me. I know that many teachers learn to teach on their own. But for new teachers in inner-city classrooms like those at the KEEP lab school, I feel this must often be an unfair and overwhelming task.

The incident in my first years of teaching that stands out in my mind has nothing to do with the teaching of reading. It occurred during my second year of teaching, when I had the kindergarten class. In November, members of the State Board of Education were to visit the KEEP lab school. At the center of the school was an observation deck with one-way mirrors allowing easy viewing of events in the three classrooms. Video cameras and microphones mounted in the ceiling of each classroom could be controlled from a panel in the observation deck as well. All the teachers at KEEP learned to observe and be observed, through the glass and on videotape. Every year we took our classes to the observation deck so the children would know that their teachers, parents, and other visitors might be watching them at any time.

As planned, members of the board were in the observation deck as I brought my class in from recess. The children had cooperated well, especially given the schedule changes made to accommodate the board's visit. Before they entered the room, I reminded the class one more time about the important visitors. The children took their seats at once, and I told them that they could now go to a learning center of their choice.

Just as the children were making their way to the various centers around the room, I heard a loud crash of keys from the piano. The children froze. I turned to see what had happened. A new student, whom I will call Tommy, stood at the piano. Tommy had just come to us from preschool with a folder two inches thick, detailing his aggressive behavior and family problems. I knew I had to do something, but I had no idea how Tommy would react. "Tommy is new to our class and he doesn't know what to do yet," I said, trying to speak in the slowest, calmest manner possible. I told the children that Tommy would be choosing a center too, and that they should just go back to what they were doing. My words seemed to hang in the air for a moment. Then the spell was broken, and the children began to move about and talk. I turned my back to Tommy and busied myself with some other children. Out of the corner of my eye, I saw Tommy go to his seat. He had a brown corduroy jacket he never removed, and he pulled the jacket up over his head and hid his face. He remained in this turtlelike position for a few minutes. Finally, he went off to one of the centers. The rest of the period passed peacefully.

After this incident, I knew that I would be able to survive as a teacher. But I learned that teaching students like those at KEEP would always be both challenging and humbling. There would be good days and bad days, and things might fall apart at any moment. I taught at the KEEP lab school in grades K–3 for 6 years, then reached the point of burnout. Nothing in my professional life has ever proved quite as demanding in either mental or emotional energy. I have great respect and admiration for the successful teachers I have come to know over the years, first in the KEEP lab school and later in Hawai'i's public schools and the Kamehameha Elementary School, who approach their teaching as a continual process of learning and self-renewal.

In my third year of teaching, I decided I needed to gain a better understanding of research on children's learning to read. At that time almost all reading research was psychological research, so I entered the master's program in psychology at the University of Hawai'i. The first semester I enrolled in a required course on animal learning; it was so difficult that half the students dropped out. The professor, M. E. (Jeff) Bitterman, an internationally known comparative psychologist, gave brilliant lectures, always without notes. I admired Jeff's manner of thinking and command of the subject and asked him to be my adviser. At the time, Jeff was conducting experiments on the learning of bees, and he pointed out that he would not be able to help me with my interest in children's learning to read. He did teach me the principles of experimental psychology, through a master's degree and all requirements for the PhD except the dissertation.

I continued to teach but participated increasingly in curriculum development and research at KEEP. Perhaps because I was a classroom teacher, I sensed the limitations in the experimental research on reading available in the 1970s; this research did not take into account the complexities of classroom life. From the beginnings of my work as a researcher, I preferred to study classroom life, particularly the work of expert teachers.

My first publication described a study of oral reading errors I had conducted with my first-grade students (Au, 1976). I found that the students could use visual-phonic (letter-sound) information but showed little skill in using context or the meaning of the sentence or passage, The results of this study, along with others conducted at KEEP, contributed to the hypothesis that the emphasis in the beginning reading instruction of Hawaiian children should be comprehension, or understanding of the text, rather than decoding. At the time, the conventional wisdom dictated that children in kindergarten through third grade should *learn to read*—that is, decode—before they *read to learn,* or read for understanding.

In 1976, as a first-grade teacher in the lab school, I taught comprehension-oriented small-group lessons for the first time. That year my students' standardized test results looked promising in comparison with those of previous classes. As a result, the next year other teachers in the lab school began to teach similar lessons. We worked from our own instincts about how to emphasize comprehension instead of decoding, by teaching the children to comprehend the stories in their basal readers. Discussions of the type we tried to hold with kindergarten through second-grade students typically did not occur in conventional reading programs until the third or fourth grade.

I began studying videotapes of small-group comprehension lessons in the fall of 1977, hoping to detect a pattern that we could turn into a systematic instructional strategy. Ron Gallimore described this as a process of moving from the unconscious to the conscious. I learned to transcribe lessons with pointers from Steve Boggs, who with Karen Watson-Gegeo was completing research on a speech event called *talk story,* which they had observed among Hawaiian children outside of school (Watson-Gegeo & Boggs, 1988).

My fellow teachers knew that I was studying comprehension instruction, and I asked them to let me know when they thought they would be teaching an interesting lesson. The teachers had a clear sense of when such lessons would occur: when they were teaching a "meaty" story, one with ideas worth discussing.

In some of the videotaped lessons, I saw that the teacher showed great skill in drawing out and developing the children's understanding of the text. In my initial analyses, I transcribed the teachers' questions. One of the most promising tapes was of a lesson taught by first-grade teacher Karen Bogert, based on the story "Jasper Makes Music." I asked Karen to take a look at the list of questions she had asked during the "Jasper" lesson. A few days later, after looking over the list, Karen told me she had had an insight. She realized that she started with a broad discussion, narrowed the focus, then opened it up again. She gave me a drawing showing her strategy; it looked like an hourglass.

In studying other lessons, I verified the pattern Karen had seen. These results became the basis for the experience-text-relationship (ETR) method (Au, 1979). When opening a lesson, teachers ask questions that bring out the children's background experiences relevant to the topic or theme of the story. Then the lessons turn to discussion of the text itself. Finally, the teacher helps the children draw relationships between the text and their own experiences. ETR lessons became an enduring feature of the KEEP curriculum.

In the 1970s the social dimensions of instruction were little understood. In my first analyses of videotapes, I became frustrated at having to distill the key points in the discussion from the welter of voices. I found it easy to transcribe the teacher's questions but extremely difficult to sort out the children's responses, because the lessons contained a tremendous amount of overlapping speech. The children were quick either to dispute or to build on one another's answers. At times their speech overlapped that of the teacher, who might have momentary difficulty getting a word in edgewise. I became preoccupied with the problem of filtering out what I thought of as the social noise from the cognitive substance of the lessons. Finally, I realized that what I had regarded as noise was actually the medium by which the children's comprehension developed. Through those rapid-fire exchanges, the students and teacher formed, questioned, and extended their shared interpretation of the story.

About this time I began to collaborate with Cathie Jordan, an anthropologist at KEEP. Cathie was interested in cultural compatibility, the idea that classroom practices should be compatible with the children's culture. While I was videotaping small-group reading lessons, Cathie was videotaping the children while they worked independently at learning centers. Her hypothesis was that the students would do well teaching and learning from one another. Because many were cared for by older sisters and brothers, they were likely to be more accustomed to learning from other children than from adults (Gallimore, Boggs, & Jordan, 1974). Drawing on the general notion of cultural compatibility, my hypothesis was that comprehension-oriented reading lessons would be more effective if conducted in a talk-story-like fashion (Au & Jordan, 1981).

In the meantime, I continued to collect videotapes. In November 1977 I arranged to videotape Claire Asam, a second-grade teacher, when she would be teaching a lesson based on a story entitled "Freddy Finds a Frog." When I viewed the tape a few days later, I was struck by the liveliness of the discussion and knew I needed to study it further. I felt sure that this tape provided a clear example of the talk-story style.

After I had been analyzing the tape for a while, I went to speak to Claire. I said I was interested in how she got the students to do so much talking. Although she did not have a label for her approach or know exactly how she did it, Claire was aware that she could turn up or limit the amount of student talk at will. She turned up the talk when she wanted to bring the ideas out of the students. She said she did not turn up the talk with all groups, because some groups were talkative anyway and did not require this approach.

I realized that what I was learning in graduate school at the University of Hawai'i was not helping me pursue the research questions I thought important. Jeff and Roland both suggested that I needed the experience of working in an active research lab where people were doing research closer to my interests. I arranged to spend the spring semester of 1978 at Rockefeller University, where Michael Cole had established the Laboratory for Comparative Human Cognition, applying in American classrooms ideas shaped by comparative research in Africa (Cole & Scribner, 1974; Scribner & Cole, 1981).

By now I had met Frederick Erickson, a noted educational anthropologist. Fred taught me the theory and method of studying participation structures, that is, the rules for speaking, listening, and turn taking as they varied within and between speech events. By applying these methods to the "Freddy" tape, I was able to confirm the talk-story hypothesis. One could not study these lessons and come away unimpressed by the speakers' intellectual and social skills. The teachers and students needed to be remarkably in tune with the rhythms of the discussion to coordinate their utterances in the rapidly shifting participation structures of the lessons.

At Rockefeller I became acquainted with Ray McDermott, who introduced me to ethnomethodology and showed me how to look at the nonverbal aspects of interaction on videotape. I also met Bill Hall, a developmental psychologist with contacts at the Center for the Study of Reading at the University of Illinois, Urbana-Champaign. Bill made it possible for me to work as a research assistant at the center, and I decided to transfer my degree work to Illinois. After a year there, I returned to Hawai'i to conduct my dissertation research on talk-story-like reading lessons. While collecting and analyzing the data, I spent my last semester as a classroom teacher.

REFLECTIONS

My attitudes toward schooling and literacy were shaped by the experiences of family members. I saw my grandmothers' longing for educational opportunities, and I have been particularly intrigued and affected by the stories of their lives. As a Chinese American with an interest in my own cultural heritage, I have explored avenues of bringing students to high levels of literacy through forms of classroom instruction respectful of their cultures.

Two findings from my work at KEEP have stayed with me over the years, and research suggests that these patterns continue to be played out in many schools serving students of diverse backgrounds. The first find-ing concerns the importance of higher-level thinking with text, specifi-cally an emphasis on reading comprehension and on the writing process. In schools serving a high proportion of students of diverse cultural and linguistic backgrounds, it is common to find an emphasis on lower-level skills, rather than higher-level thinking with text. This pattern needs to be reversed to provide students with opportunities to think deeply about the meaning of text, beginning with stories read aloud in kindergarten.

The second finding from KEEP that I have continued to pursue over time relates to the value of culturally responsive instruction. A common pattern is to find teachers relying on mainstream patterns of classroom organization and interaction (such as whole-class instruction and class-room recitation) that do not build on the strengths students bring from the home.

Reversing this pattern involves, at a minimum, providing students with small-group instruction and allowing them to participate in lessons following rules compatible with their home values.

One conclusion to be drawn from my research on talk-story-like reading lessons is that effective instruction may take more than one form. Definitions of effective teaching need to be broad enough to take into account a range of practices beyond those typically seen in main-stream settings. Another conclusion growing from my research is that students of diverse backgrounds can become excellent readers and writ-ers when they receive well-conceived, culturally responsive instruction. Conversely, the reason many students do not succeed is because they are denied high-quality instruction.

The slow acceptance of these ideas is due, I believe, to the contin-ued dominance of assimilationist ideology (Gollnick & Chinn, 2008), which leads to a narrow view of what it means to be a good student or a good teacher, deriving from a narrow view of what it means to be a good American. This narrowness also affects views of what counts as literacy, in terms of written and oral expression, mainstream and diverse cultural knowledge, standard English, and other codes.

A pluralist view of instruction takes into consideration the content of the curriculum as well as the process of instruction. I think the curricu-lum must be expanded to include time for students to explore their own cultural identities. I did not receive this opportunity in my own schooling and wish that I had. Students of diverse backgrounds will still be taught to read and write in standard English at high levels of proficiency. But they will be encouraged to use their literacy skills not just to learn mainstream content, as I did in school, but to deepen their understanding of their own worlds. We must balance the need to find common ground with the need to recognize and support the differences in culture and language that allow students of diverse backgrounds to maintain a connection to their family histories.

FOLLOW-UP ACTIVITY

Write a brief account of the origins of your own interest in schooling, literacy, or cultural diversity and have members of your class or discussion group do the same. Share your accounts, comparing and contrasting the paths that led you to the understandings you now hold.

Chapter 2

Social Constructivism and the School Literacy Learning of Students of Diverse Backgrounds

If we are serious about closing the literacy achievement gap, we must understand how the gap developed and then begin to devise solutions based on understanding these probable causes. In keeping with Key to Success #1, recognizing that the gap is complexly determined, we must have a theory about the gap and develop theoretically sound solutions.

In this chapter, I propose such a theoretical or conceptual framework for understanding and addressing the literacy achievement gap. I wrote this chapter from the perspective of social constructivism, a viewpoint that I have found to be useful not only for illuminating the challenges but for devising practical solutions. After a discussion of social constructivism, this chapter considers the explanations for the literacy achievement gap plausible from a social constructivist perspective. It argues that we must move away from a mainstream orientation to the issues and toward what I term a diverse constructivist perspective.

My work has been influenced by the thinking of Vygotsky and other social constructivist theorists. I have found social constructivism to be a powerful and generative framework for thinking about the literacy achievement gap. Social constructivism suggests that the literacy achievement gap is sustained in part through the daily interactions of teachers and students in the classroom. The actions we take as educators at the level of the school and classroom can make a difference.

I outline a comprehensive conceptual framework for addressing the literacy achievement gap, encompassing all five explanations I present. Each of the elements in this framework is explained. I discussed two of these factors in Chapter 1: culturally responsive instruction (Key to Success #3) and a curricular emphasis on higher-level thinking (Key to Success #2).

These are important factors, but others must be addressed as well if schools are to sustain high levels of literacy achievement by students and close the literacy achievement gap.

A key understanding I hope you take from this chapter is that just changing one small feature of schooling (e.g., implementing a new phonics program or a new after-school tutoring program) is only going to have limited effects. A small, specific change is not going to yield dramatic improvements in students' literacy achievement. As indicated in Key to Success #1, the literacy achievement gap is a complexly determined problem and tackling it requires a systemic approach to change, encompassing all of the factors I outline.

I am not advocating that schools attempt to tackle all of the factors at once—far from it. Schools that take on too many initiatives are seldom able to do a good job in any particular area and just end up with the same poor results for students (Au & Valencia, 2010). Instead, schools must be willing to focus and move steadily forward with a disciplined, research-based, multiyear improvement effort, a theme to which I return in Chapter 7.

I use the phrase *students of diverse backgrounds* to refer to students in the United States, usually from low-income families, who are of African American, Asian American, Latino (or Hispanic), or Native American ancestry and speak a home language other than standard American English. Differences between the school literacy achievement of these students and those of mainstream backgrounds have long been documented. The National Assessment of Educational Progress (NAEP) has compared the reading achievement of students of diverse backgrounds to that of students of mainstream backgrounds for decades, providing what appear to be the most comprehensive results on this issue. These results indicate that, although the achievement gap has narrowed since 1971, African American and Hispanic American students at all three age levels tested are not learning to read as well as their European American peers (Rampey, Dion, & Donahue, 2009).

The gap between the school literacy achievement of students of diverse backgrounds and those of mainstream backgrounds is a cause of growing concern, especially given demographic trends. Urban school districts in particular are faced with the task of educating an increasing number of students of diverse cultural and linguistic backgrounds from families living in poverty (Pallas, Natriello, & McDill, 1989).

From the perspective of social constructivism, it may be argued that both success and failure in literacy learning are the collaborative social accomplishments of school systems, communities, teachers, students, and families (e.g., McDermott & Gospodinoff, 1981). The thesis to be developed is that a social constructivist perspective on literacy achievement of students of diverse backgrounds can be strengthened by moving from a mainstream orientation to an orientation toward diversity, giving greater consideration to issues of ethnicity, primary language, and social class (see also Reyes, 1991a). Although issues of gender play an important role, a discussion of these issues and feminist perspectives is beyond the scope of this chapter.

To develop the argument for a diverse constructivist perspective, I discuss social constructivism and its application to research on school literacy learning. Then I outline what appear to be the major explanations, consistent with a social constructivist position, for the achievement gap between students of diverse backgrounds and those of mainstream backgrounds. Finally, I propose a conceptual framework for improving the school literacy learning of students of diverse backgrounds. In discussing this framework, I review concerns about the largely mainstream nature of the constructivist orientation as applied to issues of school literacy learning and instruction and highlight the implications of taking a diverse constructivist orientation toward these issues.

SOCIAL CONSTRUCTIVISM

At the heart of constructivism is a concern for lived experience, or the world as it is felt and understood by social actors (Schwandt, 1994). Constructivists reject the naive realism of the positivists, the critical realism of the postpositivists, and the historical realism of the critical theorists, in favor of a relativism based on multiple mental constructions formulated by groups and individuals (Guba & Lincoln, 1994). There are many forms of constructivism, which appear to differ along several dimensions, including the relative importance of human communities versus the individual learner in the construction of knowledge (Phillips, 1995).

Spivey (1997) presented a detailed treatment of constructivism and its influence on contemporary literacy research. She noted that, in constructivism, communication or discourse processes are compared to processes of building, and generative acts, such as those of interpreting or composing texts, tend to be emphasized. Themes in constructivist work

include active engagement in processes of meaning making, text comprehension as a window on these processes, and the varied nature of knowledge, especially knowledge developed as a consequence of membership
in a given social group. In exploring different conceptions of constructivism, Spivey highlights the issue of agency, and whether the focus is seen
as the individual, small groups and dyads, or communities and societies.

Both sociology and psychology have undergone a transformation
from views of constructivism centered on the personal, subjective nature
of knowledge construction to views centered on its social, intersubjective
nature (Mehan, 1981). These newer views are generally called *social constructivism*. The social is seen to encompass a wide range of phenomena,
from historical, political, and cultural trends to face-to-face interactions,
reflecting group processes, both explicit and implicit, with intended and
unintended consequences. In the case of literacy research, the social can
include historical changes in definitions of literacy, functions and uses of
literacy within communities, and the social construction of success and
failure in learning to read in school, to name a few.

Social constructivists argue that the very terms by which people
perceive and describe the world, including language, are social artifacts
(Schwandt, 1994). Because reality is seen to be created through processes
of social exchange, historically situated, social constructivists are interested
in the collective generation of meaning among people. Social constructivism includes the idea that there is no objective basis for knowledge claims,
because knowledge is always a human construction. The emphasis is on the
process of knowledge construction by the social group and the intersubjec-
tivity established through the interactions of the group.

Vygotsky (1987) is the theorist who appears to have had the greatest
influence on literacy researchers working from a social constructivist perspective. Social, cultural, and historical factors all play a part in Vygotsky's
theory of cognitive development. Vygotsky saw the focus of psychology as
the study of consciousness or mind, and he wanted to discover how higher
or "artificial" mental functions developed from the "natural" psychological functions that emerged through maturation. A *higher mental function*,
such as literacy, is an aspect of human behavior, present in some form from
man's beginnings, that has changed over time as a result of cumulative historical experience (Cole & Griffin, 1983). Vygotsky's view of consciousness included two subcomponents, intellect and affect, which he regarded
as inseparable (Wertsch, 1985). Social constructivist research on literacy

includes attention to the motivational and emotional dimensions of literacy, as well as the cognitive and strategic ones.

Vygotsky's approach to learning was holistic, and he advocated the study of higher mental functions with all their complexity (Moll, 1990). He argued for research on units with all the basic characteristics of the whole and rejected methods based on the analysis of separate elements. Similarly, research on school literacy learning conducted from a social constructivist perspective assumes that students need to engage in authentic literacy activities, not activities contrived for practice.

Vygotsky believed that the internalization of higher mental functions involved the transfer from the interpsychological to the intrapsychological, that is, from socially supported to individually controlled performance. Perhaps the best known of Vygotsky's formulations is the *zone of proximal development,* by which he sought to explain the social origin of higher mental functions. He defined the zone as the "difference between the child's actual level of development and the level of performance that he achieves in collaboration with the adult" (Vygotsky, 1987, p. 209). Social constructivist research on literacy learning focuses on the role of teachers, peers, and family members in mediating learning, on the dynamics of classroom instruction, and on the organization of systems within which children learn or fail to learn (Moll, 1990).

Everyday and *scientific* concepts are differentiated in Vygotsky's (1987) theory. The child gains everyday (or spontaneous) concepts through daily life, whereas she learns scientific concepts through formal instruction and schooling. In Vygotsky's view, the two kinds of concepts are joined in the process of development, each contributing to the growth of the other. Research conducted from a social constructivist perspective addresses the manner in which school literacy learning activities can be restructured to allow students to acquire academic knowledge (scientific concepts) by building on the foundation of personal experience (everyday concepts). Or, conversely, this research looks at how students may gain insights into their own lives through the application of academic knowledge.

Vygotsky argued that higher mental processes are always mediated by signs and tools or instruments. Wertsch (1990) pointed out that signs and tools, in Vygotsky's view, do not simply facilitate activity but shape and define it in fundamental ways. Obviously, language and writing systems are foremost among the cultural tools developed by and available to people in different societies. The forms of language and literacy within each culture have developed over time to carry the concepts that reflect the experience of that cultural group. Thus the historical condition is joined to the cultural condition, and links among historical, cultural, and individual conditions are formed when children are learning to use language and literacy. In the next section, I draw on a social constructivist perspective and the ideas of Vygotsky in providing an overview of explanations for the literacy achievement gap.

EXPLANATIONS FOR THE ACHIEVEMENT GAP

From a social constructivist perspective, research should account for the literacy achievement gap in terms of the societal conditions that led to its creation and sustain it over time, through students' daily interactions and experiences in school. As shown in Figure 2.1, five major explanations appear plausible from a social constructivist perspective. I arrived at this scheme of explanatory categories through a process that involved first, identifying what appeared to be the major lines of educational research, consistent with a social constructivist viewpoint, that attempt to account for the achievement gap. Second, I drew on the explanatory categories proposed by other researchers (e.g., Jacob & Jordan, 1993; Strickland & Ascher, 1992).

The first explanatory category is that of *linguistic differences* and stems from the fact that many students of diverse backgrounds speak a home language other than standard American English (e.g., the home language of many Latino students is Spanish). Current theory and research in bilingual education, consistent with a social constructivist perspective, suggest that students' poor academic achievement generally is not due to their limited English proficiency. Rather, it is due to the exclusion or limited use of instruction in the home language in many school programs (Snow, 1990) or to the low status accorded the home language. Unlike mainstream students, students of diverse backgrounds are not encouraged to use their existing language skills as the basis for developing literacy in school, because these skills often are ignored or denigrated (Moll & Diaz, 1985). For example, Spanish-speaking students may be prevented from expressing in Spanish their thoughts about a story with an English text. Thus linguistic differences are related to decreased opportunity to use existing language skills as the foundation for learning to read and write.

Figure 2.1. Explanations for the Literacy Achievement Gap

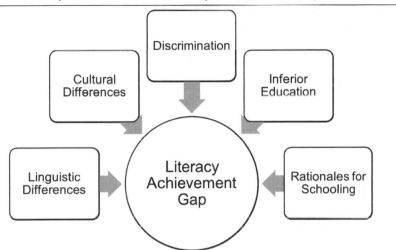

A second explanatory category is that of *cultural differences*. Proponents of this position attribute the lack of school success experienced by many students of diverse backgrounds to their preference for forms of interaction, language, and thought that conflict with the mainstream behaviors generally needed for success in school (Au & Mason, 1981; Philips, 1972). These preferences are not inborn but the result of socialization practices in the home and community, which in turn reflect cultural values. Because the school is a mainstream institution, instruction is carried out in ways following mainstream standards for behavior and reflecting mainstream cultural values. Students have difficulty learning in school because instruction does not follow their community's cultural values and standards for behavior. For example, Au and Mason (1981) found that Native Hawaiian students performed poorly in reading lessons, showing a considerable degree of inattentiveness, when teachers conducted these lessons following the rules for conventional classroom recitation. These students paid more attention to reading, discussed more text ideas, and made more logical inferences about the text when their reading lessons were conducted in a culturally responsive manner. In the culturally responsive lessons the teacher allowed the students to follow rules for participation much like those in talk story, a common speech event in the Hawaiian community. In talk-story-like reading lessons, unlike classroom recitation, the students could collaborate in producing responses and there was a high degree of overlapping speech.

A third explanatory category is that of *discrimination* (also called societal racism; Strickland & Ascher, 1992). From a social constructivist perspective, it can be argued that poverty and school failure are both manifestations of historical and systemic conditions rooted in discrimination. The argument is that American society and its system of schooling are structured to prevent equality of educational opportunity and outcome. For example, disproportionate numbers of students of diverse backgrounds are labeled as poor readers and placed in the lowest reading groups in the classroom or sent from the classroom to receive remedial reading instruction. The instruction these students receive is qualitatively different from that of students placed in higher groups and tends to further hinder their learning to read. Shannon (1989) summarized research suggesting that low-group students receive the message that reading does not have to make sense, that accurate pronunciation is more important than comprehension, and that they need not be responsible for monitoring their own reading.

The fourth explanatory category suggests that differences in academic achievement are due to the *inferior education* received by students of diverse backgrounds (Strickland & Ascher, 1992). For example, urban schools with a high proportion of African American students frequently have deteriorating buildings, outdated textbooks, inexperienced teachers, and surroundings that expose students to violence. Material circumstances in these schools and in the conditions of students' lives and communities lead to "savage inequalities" in educational opportunity (Kozol, 1991). Schools with a high proportion of low-income students tend to devote less time to reading instruction and to rely on testing practices that limit students' opportunities to learn (Allington, 1991).

A fifth explanatory category highlights the importance of *rationales for schooling*. D'Amato (1987) noted that students who accept school and cooperate with teachers do so on the basis of rationales related to either the structural or situational implications of school. *Structural rationales* involve children's understanding of the significance of school performances to settings beyond the school, such as their relationship to employment and other life opportunities. Structural rationales allow students of mainstream backgrounds to justify their participation in school, because they usually have family histories illustrating a strong connection between schooling and life opportunities. However, structural rationales usually are not available to students of diverse backgrounds whose family histories do not show these same connections (Ogbu, 1981). *Situational rationales* are found in students' experiences with being in school and whether or not that experience is rewarding and enjoyable. Situational rationales for accepting school are available to children when school structures and processes are compatible with the structures and processes of their peer groups (D'Amato, 1988). D'Amato argues that schools cannot rely on structural rationales but must make situational rationales available to students of diverse backgrounds as a way of motivating them to remain in school.

Considerable research supports all five of these explanations, a testimony to the complexity of the issues. Yet researchers have tended to focus on one explanatory category or another in their attempts to account for achievement differences. Few steps have been taken toward developing a comprehensive explanation of the achievement gap by simultaneously considering the contributions of research associated with different explanatory categories.

CUMMINS'S THEORETICAL FRAMEWORK

A conceptual framework for improving the literacy achievement of students of diverse backgrounds should seek to bring together the various explanations described above and show their application to school literacy learning in particular. A starting point can be found in the work of Cummins (1986), who proposed a theoretical framework for empowering students of diverse backgrounds, as shown in Figure 2.2. His framework is consistent with a social constructivist perspective in its recognition of the links between events in the school and conditions in the larger society, the centrality of the teacher's role in mediating learning, the inseparability of affective or motivational factors and academic achievement, and the connections between schooled knowledge and personal experience. Cummins's framework has the virtue of incorporating all five explanations, and for this reason provides an appropriate organizational structure for the diverse constructivist framework proposed here.

The concept of empowerment is central to Cummins's framework. Cummins views empowerment as both a mediating construct and an outcome variable. Empowered students are confident in their own cultural

Literacy Achievement and Diversity

Figure 2.2. Cummins's Theoretical Framework

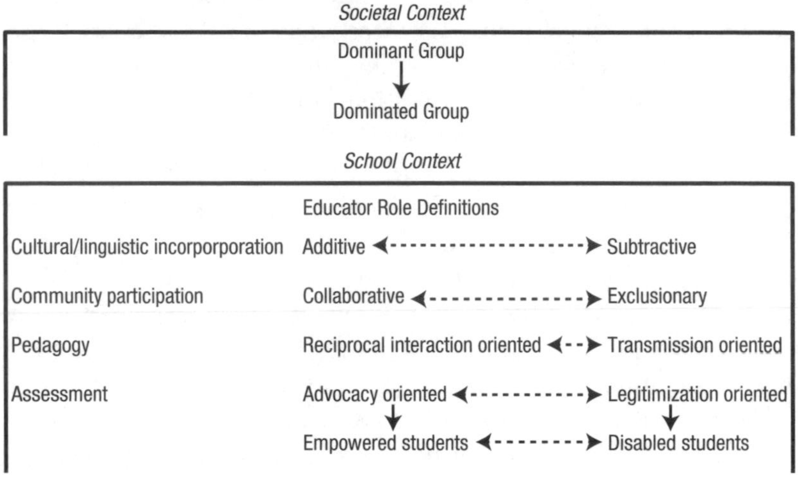

Societal Context

Dominant Group

↓

Dominated Group

School Context

Educator Role Definitions

Cultural/linguistic incorporporation	Additive ◄------------------► Subtractive
Community participation	Collaborative ◄-------------► Exclusionary
Pedagogy	Reciprocal interaction oriented ◄--► Transmission oriented
Assessment	Advocacy oriented ◄----------► Legitimization oriented
	Empowered students ◄--------► Disabled students

Source: From Cummins, J. (1986). Empowering Minority Students: A Framework for Intervention. *Harvard Educational Review, 56,* p. 24. Copyright © 1986 by the President and Fellows of Harvard College. Adapted with permission.

identity, as well as knowledgeable of school structures and interactional patterns, and so can participate successfully in school learning activities. Cummins (1994) distinguishes between coercive and collaborative relations of power. Coercive relations of power legitimate the subordinate status of students of diverse backgrounds, on the assumption that there is a fixed amount of power, so that the sharing of power with other groups will necessarily decrease the status of the dominant group. In collaborative relations of power, no group is put above others, and power is not fixed in quantity, because it is assumed to be generated in the interactions among groups and individuals. The nature of relations of power, whether coercive or collaborative, within the larger society leads to the development of educational structures that shape the interactions among educators and students in schools. These interactions determine whether the zone of proximal development is constituted so as to help students think for themselves or accept the existing social order. Particular formulations of the zone thus contribute to students' empowerment or disempowerment.

The interactions between students and educators are mediated by the role definitions that educators assume. In Cummins's (1986) framework these role definitions were seen to be influenced by three social contexts:

(1) power relations among groups within the society as a whole, (2) relationships between schools and diverse communities, and (3) interactions between teachers and students in the classroom. Cummins urged an examination of dominant/subordinate group issues, as discussed by critical theorists, because of apparent parallels between the way students of diverse backgrounds are disabled by schools and the way their communities are disempowered by forces in the larger society. He argued that the academic success of students of diverse backgrounds depends upon the extent to which patterns of interaction in the school reverse those in the larger society.

Cummins suggested that, if students of diverse backgrounds are to be empowered in school, educators must redefine their roles and assumptions in four key structural elements. For each element the role definitions of educators are seen to lie along a continuum, with definitions at one end tending to disable students, and definitions at the other tending to empower them. The first element has to do with the incorporation of the language and culture of students of diverse backgrounds in the school program. The second element is concerned with the extent to which the involvement of community members is an integral part of the school's program. The third element refers to pedagogy that encourages students of diverse backgrounds to use language to construct their own knowledge. The fourth element, assessment, addresses the extent to which educators tend to label or disable students of diverse backgrounds, as opposed to serving as advocates for them.

Through a consideration of larger, societal influences on school and through these four elements, Cummins provides a comprehensive framework for empowering students of diverse backgrounds. Yet this framework is not without weaknesses. From the perspective of critical theory, this framework can be faulted for focusing more on the roles of educators than on issues of power in the larger society that constrain the actions of both educators and students. Another possible criticism is that Cummins's framework does not address the material circumstances with which teachers and students must contend, as illustrated in the work of Kozol (1991).

PROPOSED CONCEPTUAL FRAMEWORK

The proposed framework for improving the school literacy learning of students of diverse backgrounds is shown in Figure 2.3. The seven elements in the framework reflect key areas of research on school literacy learning,

Figure 2.3. Proposed Conceptual Framework

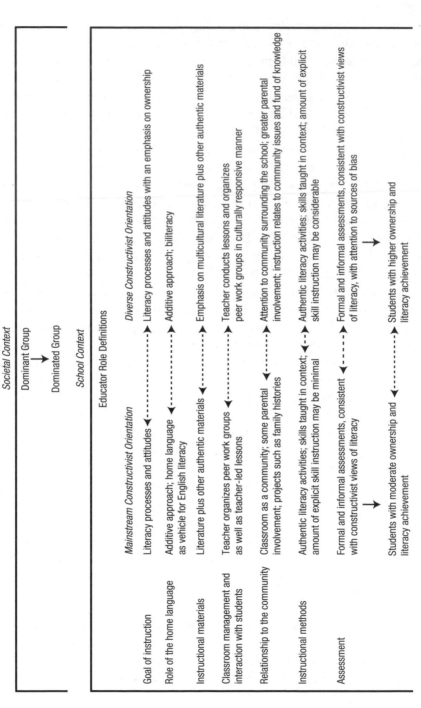

Source: From Cummins, J. (1986). Empowering Minority Students: A Framework for Intervention. *Harvard Educational Review, 56,* p. 24. Copyright © 1986 by the President and Fellows of Harvard College. Adapted with permission.

especially that conducted by scholars from underrepresented groups. This research and the framework are consistent with the assumptions of social constructivism outlined earlier in this chapter. The framework attempts to capture the strengths of the five explanations for the literacy achievement gap and incorporates many of the features of Cummins's framework, although it focuses on school literacy learning in particular rather than student empowerment in general. Whereas Cummins's framework has four elements, the proposed framework requires seven in order to incorporate the major areas of literacy research I identified. The seven elements are the goal of instruction, the role of the home language, instructional materials, classroom management and interaction with students, relationship to the community, instructional methods, and assessment.

One end of the continuum represents what I call a mainstream constructivist orientation and the other, a diverse constructivist orientation. I see differences between the mainstream and diverse constructivist orientations as a matter of emphasis and degree rather than kind. I take the position that the social constructivist orientation can serve well to address issues of the school literacy learning of students of diverse backgrounds. However, an adequate treatment of these issues requires that discussions move beyond the boundaries usually evident in mainstream interpretations of social constructivism. In my opinion, a mainstream constructivist orientation does not take adequate account of differences in ethnicity, primary language, and social class that may affect students' school literacy learning.

A diverse constructivist orientation attempts to look at how schools devalue, and could revalue, the cultural capital of students of diverse backgrounds (Bourdieu & Passeron, 1977). For the revaluing process to take place, educators can experiment with collaborative power relations that do not privilege mainstream knowledge claims over the knowledge claims of students of diverse backgrounds. A mainstream constructivist orientation recognizes that students' knowledge claims must be considered valid within students' own cultural contexts. A diverse constructivist orientation takes this line of reasoning one step further, by inquiring into the ways that knowledge claims, of educators and their students, are related to cultural identity and shaped by ethnicity, primary language, and social class. The experiences students bring to literacy events (e.g., the forms of their narratives) may depart significantly from educators' expectations. The revaluing process includes teachers' acceptance of students as cultural beings. It also encompasses the manner in which teachers receive and extend students' literacy efforts and encourage students to interact with peers and with texts.

A mainstream constructivist orientation tends to assume that similarities among students override differences related to ethnicity, primary language, and social class. In a mainstream constructivist orientation the tendency is to propose general principles applicable to all students, although individual differences may be considered. This point of view fails to acknowledge that a given set of learning opportunities may benefit mainstream students while working to the detriment of students of diverse backgrounds within the same classroom. A diverse constructivist perspective assumes that general principles must be examined and refined so that their specific application to local contexts involving particular groups of children can be understood. Investigations include the possible influences of ethnicity, primary language, and social class on students' responses to particular literacy learning activities and the reshaping of these activities to improve students' opportunities to learn.

Educators' recognition of the inequities possible in a given educational situation depends on an understanding of their own cultural identities as well as the cultural identities of their students. Researchers, too, should be aware of how their cultural identities shape their studies of literacy and literacy learning, in terms of research questions, methodologies, relationships with participants, and attention paid to the consequences of their work. Research conducted from a diverse constructivist orientation addresses issues of educators' and students' cultural identities, and the specific ways in which ethnicity, primary language, and social class may interact in school settings that can be effective or ineffective in bringing students of diverse backgrounds to high levels of literacy. Often, the goal of this research is not merely to describe but to improve the education of students of diverse backgrounds (Moll & Diaz, 1987).

In a mainstream constructivist orientation it may be assumed that students primarily need to acquire the proficiency in literacy needed for self-expression and for success in the larger society. From a diverse constructivist orientation it can be suggested that a concern for proficiency should not be allowed to override a concern for the transformative possibilities of literacy, both for the individual and for the society. Garrison (1995) referred to the double bind: "the tension between the need of the students to appropriate historically entrenched tools that empower them as social actors and the simultaneous need of the culture to retool and recreate itself" (p. 729). Literacy is one such tool. With students of diverse backgrounds conventional school literacy practices may serve as instruments of control and disempowerment, superseding and displacing the literacy practices of students' families and communities. The double bind in this instance is that current societal conditions and school practices make it difficult for students of diverse backgrounds to attain the high levels of literacy that would enable them to reflect on, critique, and address situations of inequity. Yet by virtue of their positioning with respect to ethnicity, language, and class, these students might represent the very viewpoints needed to reshape the society in significant ways.

To overcome the barriers of exclusion posed by conventional literacy instructional practices, educators must work with an expanded vision of literacy strategies and concepts in school, so that school definitions of literacy are transformed. In this way, educators create the possibility, not only of helping students become proficient in literacy, but of enabling them to be empowered through literacy, to use literacy as a tool in bettering societal conditions.

The proposed framework follows that of Cummins in indicating that educator role definitions are embedded within and influenced by three social contexts: the larger society, including the power relations among groups; the school and the diverse communities it serves; and the classroom, including the interactions between teachers and students. The manner in which the framework incorporates the various explanations for the achievement gap is described below, as each of the seven elements is addressed in turn. The propositions are intended as ideas to be explored, not as final solutions. They grow not only from the research base but from my experience over a period of 25 years in classrooms with Native Hawaiian children, which includes research with teachers encompassing each of the propositions below (e.g., Au & Carroll, 1997).

Goal of Instruction

Proposition: The school literacy learning of students of diverse backgrounds will be improved as educators establish students' ownership of literacy as the overarching goal of the language arts curriculum. This proposition builds on the notion of empowerment (Cummins, 1994). Ownership, in this case the notion that literacy is personally meaningful and viewed as useful for the individual's own purposes, is seen as both a mediating construct and an outcome variable, just as empowerment has both these roles in Cummins's framework.

Educators with a mainstream constructivist orientation generally define literacy in terms of students' attitudes, such as enjoyment of reading and writing, as well as in terms of cognitive processes, such as those for revising a piece of writing. However, often associated with the mainstream constructivist orientation is a reluctance to focus on particular outcomes or to give priority to any particular instructional goals. This reluctance appears to grow from the view that a focus on outcomes or goals is inconsistent with the holistic nature of literacy and literacy learning and may lead to a narrowing of instruction (e.g., Goodman, 1992).

My own view of this issue is that educators with a diverse constructivist orientation should give priority to students' ownership of literacy. Ownership is recognized in process approaches to be important for all students (Dudley-Marling & Searle, 1995). However, I argue that it should be the major consideration or overarching goal in literacy curricula for students of diverse backgrounds (see Chapter 5). This argument is grounded in D'Amato's (1987) research on the role of situational rationales, discussed earlier. An explicit statement that ownership is the overarching goal has the advantage of reminding educators that literacy must be made personally meaningful to students of diverse backgrounds. Educators who wish to make literacy personally meaningful to students consistently draw on students' interests and experiences. By making literacy activities rewarding in an immediate sense, they provide students with the situational rationales for staying in school and engaging in literacy learning.

It should be noted that ownership in and of itself seems to be a necessary but not a sufficient condition for promoting the school literacy learning of students of diverse backgrounds. A study of an innovative constructivist literacy curriculum in classrooms with Hawaiian students indicated that most developed ownership of literacy, as operationally defined by the assessment measures (Au, 1994). However, high levels of ownership were not necessarily associated with high levels of reading comprehension and composition. In classrooms where teachers view ownership as the overarching goal, attention must still be paid to systematic instruction in the cognitive processes of reading and writing. An extensive discussion of students' ownership of literacy is provided in Chapter 5.

Role of the Home Language

Proposition: The school literacy learning of students of diverse backgrounds will improve as educators recognize the importance of students' home languages and come to see biliteracy as an attainable and desirable outcome. This proposition relates to the linguistic differences explanation and to Cummins's notion of cultural/linguistic incorporation.

Educators with a mainstream constructivist orientation usually take an additive approach. They believe that schools should add to and build on strengths in students' home languages, and they understand the value of literacy instruction in these languages. The assumption is that one only needs to learn to read and write once, and that this learning is transferable to another language (Weber, 1991).

Educators with a diverse constructivist orientation concur with these views and argue further that literacy in the home language should not be treated simply as a means for becoming literate in English. Rather, literacy in the home language should be valued in and of itself, just as literacy in a foreign language is valued at the college level. Unlike those with a mainstream orientation, educators with a diverse constructivist orientation often support *biliteracy*, the ability to read and write in two languages, the home language and English. Research suggests that the greater problem lies in the maintenance and development of skills in the home language rather than in students' learning of English (Pease-Alvarez & Hakuta, 1992). When biliteracy is the goal, students have the chance to use and extend literacy in the home language even after they have become literate in English

Instructional Materials

Proposition: The school literacy learning of students of diverse backgrounds will improve as educators use materials that present diverse cultures in an authentic manner, especially through the works of authors of diverse backgrounds. This element relates to the cultural differences and inferior education explanations and to the element of cultural/linguistic incorporation in Cummins's framework.

Educators with a mainstream constructivist orientation advocate the use of literature for reading instruction. They argue that the reading of literature provides students with richer, more interesting, and more motivating reading experiences. In a study conducted by Morrow (1992), students of diverse backgrounds who participated in a literature-based program outperformed control group students on a variety of literacy and language measures, including those for comprehension, story retelling, and story rewriting.

Educators with a diverse constructivist orientation share this view of the importance of literature, but extend it by arguing for the inclusion of multicultural literature. In particular, educators with a diverse constructivist orientation endorse the use of multicultural works, usually by authors of diverse backgrounds, that present cultures in an authentic manner (Harris, 1992). The use of literature that accurately depicts the experiences of diverse groups may improve the literacy achievement of students of diverse backgrounds by increasing their motivation to read (Spears-Bunton, 1990), their appreciation and understanding of their own language and cultural heritage (Jordan, 1988), and their valuing of their own life experience as a topic for writing. Carol Lee (1991) found that African American students, who were considered below-average readers, could write insightful interpretations of the significance of the color purple in Alice Walker's (1982) novel.

When using multicultural literature, educators with a diverse constructivist orientation recognize that attention must be given not only to the selection of books but also to the curricular approach. Rasinski and Padak (1990) used Banks's (1989) hierarchy of approaches in multicultural education to define different approaches for the use of multicultural literature, including the transformation and social action approaches. Teachers who follow these approaches use multicultural literature to promote critical analysis of social and historical issues and to empower students to work on the resolution of social problems.

Classroom Management and Interactions with Students

Proposition: The school literacy learning of students of diverse backgrounds will improve as educators become culturally responsive in their management of classrooms and interactions with students. This element relates to the cultural differences explanation and the rationales for schooling explanation, as well as to the element of cultural/linguistic incorporation in Cummins's framework.

Educators with a mainstream constructivist orientation see genuine literacy activities, over which students can feel ownership, as central to classroom organization and management (Routman, 1991). These educators recognize that students may learn effectively not only in teacher-led lessons but through collaboration with peers. Discussions of literature may take the form of grand conversations (Eeds & Wells, 1989), and these conversations may have rules more like those for everyday talk than for classroom recitation.

Educators with a diverse constructivist orientation agree with the spirit of these innovations but point out that the teacher's approach to classroom management and interaction with students may need to be adjusted on the basis of differences in students' cultures. Delpit (1988) cited the expectation of African American students that the teacher act like an authority figure, displaying authority in a more direct and explicit manner than a mainstream teacher might. The authoritative teacher establishes a high standard of achievement, demands that students reach that standard, and holds students' attention by using features of Black communicative style (Foster, 1989). Considerable research has been conducted on culturally responsive instruction (for reviews, see Au & Kawakami, 1994; Osborne, 1996). This research suggests that students' opportunities to learn to read improve when teachers conduct lessons in a culturally responsive manner, consistent with community values and norms for interaction.

Relationship to the Community

Proposition: The school literacy learning of students of diverse backgrounds will be improved as educators make stronger links to the community. This proposition builds on the idea of community participation in Cummins's framework. It relates to the discrimination explanation in pointing to the need to restructure power relations between the school and community, and to the cultural differences explanation in highlight ing how the involvement of parents and other community members in the schools may increase the cultural and linguistic relevance of school situations for students of diverse backgrounds.

Educators with a mainstream constructivist orientation describe classrooms as communities of learners but do not often extend the concept of community beyond the school (Barrera, 1992). They are concerned about informing and educating parents about their children's activities in constructivist-oriented classrooms and ask parents to assist with such tasks as the publishing of the children's writing (Routman, 1991). Students write memoirs, and these projects frequently involve them in interactions with family members (Whitin, 1990).

Educators with a diverse constructivist orientation support all of these activities but go a step further. They point to the notion that literacy practices, as well as the resources available to promote literacy, differ across cultures, and that connections need to be made to the specific communities to which students belong. For example, Taylor and Dorsey-Gaines (1988) discovered a deep valuing of literacy in the homes of young African

American children growing up in poverty but the absence of a connection between the children's literacy experiences at home and at school. Students' school literacy learning would have been strengthened if connections to home literacy practices had been made. Moll (1992) described the "funds of knowledge" present among Mexican American households and how teachers motivated students to write about topics such as building and city planning, using parents and other community members as speakers. In the Home Literacy Project, Edwards (2009) demonstrated the benefits to students' literacy learning of collaboration between the home and school.

Instructional Methods

Proposition: The school literacy learning of students of diverse backgrounds will be improved as educators provide students with both authentic literacy activities and a considerable amount of instruction in the specific literacy skills needed for full participation in the culture of power. This proposition relates to the discrimination and inferior education explanations, and to the pedagogy element in Cummins's framework.

Although educators with a mainstream constructivist orientation provide students with authentic literacy activities, the amount of skill instruction in the context of these activities may vary considerably. Because the emphasis in constructivist approaches tends to be on process rather than product, educators with a mainstream constructivist orientation may see it as their role to act as facilitators of students' learning, responding to students' work but not transmitting knowledge (Reyes, 1991b). Educators with this orientation may be reluctant to provide students with instruction on specific skills. However, a countervailing tendency is evident, as seen in Spiegel's (1992) work on the blending of whole language and systematic direct instruction.

Educators with a diverse constructivist perspective agree that skills should be taught within the context of authentic literacy activities. They appear to depart from the mainstream constructivist perspective in their views about the nature and degree of teacher mediation required to promote the literacy learning of students of diverse backgrounds. In a study of the literacy learning of bilingual Latino students, Reyes (1991b) concluded that students' progress appeared to depend on a higher degree of teacher mediation and scaffolding than their process-oriented teacher felt she should provide. Delpit (1988) argued that students of diverse backgrounds are outsiders to the culture of power and deserve to gain a command of conventions and forms of discourse already known to insiders (those of mainstream backgrounds). She distinguished between what she called personal literacy and power code literacy. Although both are important, it is the latter that is needed for success in the larger society. The knotty issues of skill instruction and the literacy learning of students of diverse backgrounds are discussed in detail in Chapter 6.

Assessment

Proposition: The school literacy learning of students of diverse backgrounds will be improved when educators use forms of assessment that eliminate or reduce sources of bias (such as prior knowledge, language, and question type) and more accurately reflect students' literacy achievement. This proposition relates to the inferior education explanation and to the assessment element in Cummins's framework.

Educators with a mainstream constructivist perspective have at times contributed to the development of alternative forms of assessment, including portfolios and statewide tests such as those implemented in Michigan and Illinois in the late 1980s. These assessments were consistent with current views of literacy in focusing on the process of meaning construction (Pearson & Valencia, 1987).

Educators with a diverse constructivist orientation support the development of alternatives to standardized testing. However, they recognize that innovative approaches to assessment also have the potential to work to the detriment of students of diverse backgrounds. For example, performance-based assessments tied to standards may not be sufficiently flexible to assess the literacy of Spanish-speaking children. If innovative assessments are high-stakes in nature, poor performance may carry the same negative consequences associated with standardized testing. These educators recognize that all forms of assessment, whether formal or informal, may incorporate elements of bias (Garcia & Pearson, 1991). Garcia (1991) compared the reading test performance of bilingual Latino students in the fifth and sixth grades with that of monolingual European American students in the same classrooms. She found that the tests underestimated the reading comprehension of the Latino students, because of their having less prior knowledge of the topics in passages and a tendency to apply strategies of literal interpretation to questions with textually implicit answers. Langer, Bartolome, Vasquez, and Lucas (1990) explored ways of tapping the text comprehension of bilingual fifth graders. One of their findings was that open-ended *envisionment* questions (e.g., What have you learned that is happening so far?) elicited more information from students than decontextualized probing questions (e.g., What order was used in the piece you just read?).

In presenting this framework I do not propose a process-product relationship, in a positivist sense, between any particular proposition or element and students' literacy achievement. All elements will operate in the context of schools and classrooms in which larger social, political, and economic forces, such as those explored by the critical theorists, play an important part. Educational change may well be prevented by material circumstances or stifled by policy decisions. Or change may take place with results that fail to be recognized, as in situations where standardized test scores are the only sanctioned outcomes. Furthermore, the complexity of school situations makes it impossible to isolate the possible effects of any single element or group of elements, and elements may interact in complex ways. Still, the overall implication is that the school literacy learning of students of diverse backgrounds will be stronger in schools and classrooms where elements of a diverse constructivist orientation are in place than in settings where they are not.

CONCLUSION

The thrust of this chapter has been to argue for the need to move from a mainstream to diverse constructivist orientation in research on the literacy achievement gap between students of diverse backgrounds and students of mainstream backgrounds. Taking a diverse constructivist perspective and in keeping with Key to Success #1, I presented a framework incorporating multiple explanations for the literacy achievement gap and suggested researchable actions that might be taken in schools. In concluding, I step away from the framework itself to reflect on sources of tension evident in discussions of the literacy achievement of students of diverse backgrounds, and certainly in this chapter as well.

A first source of tension arises from the ontological, epistemological, and methodological differences between the competing paradigms of constructivism and critical theory (Guba & Lincoln, 1994; for a discussion of epistemological issues and reading research, see Shannon, 1989). These tensions are evident in the very framing of the problem of the literacy achievement gap: what the gap signifies and what steps should be taken to address it. Without crossing from one paradigm to the other, it is difficult to link micro- and macrolevels of analyses, necessary to an understanding of how relations of power in the larger society play out in the way literacy instruction is organized and enacted in schools and classrooms. At the same time, attempts to incorporate critical notions into a constructivist framework, or the reverse, are likely to appear inconsistent when judged from the perspective of one paradigm or the other. I do not think these tensions can or should be resolved, but it seems desirable to have a principled importing of ideas across paradigms, as is taking place in educational anthropology.

A related source of tension arises because of differences in the political ideologies associated with liberalism and radicalism. No doubt, some will prefer a framework oriented toward more ambitious ends than those proposed here. As a researcher with liberal leanings, I am persuaded that all research is inherently political (Kincheloe & McLaren, 2000), but I do not see a research agenda and a political agenda as one and the same. As a school-oriented researcher, I have constantly been reminded of the difference between what I see as a desired end and the increment of benefit to students and teachers that seems possible under the circumstances. Extending this view to the proposed framework, I incorporated elements that seemed researchable and achievable, at least in some school settings.

Still another source of tension resides in the differing perspectives of mainstream researchers and researchers from underrepresented groups. As I reviewed the literature, it became clear that many of the criticisms of the mainstream constructivist orientation had been formulated by researchers from underrepresented groups. This I see as no accident. These researchers may provide an insider's perspective on issues of literacy achievement with students of diverse backgrounds, through a deep understanding of issues of ethnicity, primary language, and social class gained through personal as well as professional experience. In discussions of the literacy achievement gap their work deserves more attention than it presently seems to receive, perhaps because of a tendency to downplay the value of studies conducted by these researchers of issues within their own communities (Frierson, 1990).

A final source of tension lies between the world of the academy and the world of the school and centers on whether researchers should keep a distance from, or be participants in, the situations being studied (Reason, 1994). Analyzing the problem is, of course, quite different from working on solutions in collaboration with educators in schools. In evaluating the contributions of critical theory to education, Giroux (1989) suggested that too much emphasis has been placed on the language of critique, too little on the language of possibility. Critical theorists, he noted, have been so concerned with the existing realities of schools that they have failed to address the question of what school should be. In a similar vein, Delpit (1991) and Ladson-Billings (1994) called for more research on situations in which students of diverse backgrounds are experiencing academic success. We are reminded, then, that the greater challenge is not in proposing frameworks but in bringing about changes in schools that will close the literacy achievement gap. In Chapter 7 I discuss my experiences in seeking to meet this challenge.

FOLLOW-UP ACTIVITY

Make a list of the seven elements in the framework. Add notes indicating what your school, or a school that you know well, is doing to address each of these elements. Devise a multiyear plan indicating how the school might move forward with each of these elements over time.

Chapter 3

Culturally Responsive Instruction: Application to Multiethnic Classrooms

We live in an era of rapid change when the pressures of globalization are spurring nations to push their standards for literacy ever higher. In this context I believe we must be concerned that the movement toward higher standards could lead over time to a widening of the literacy achievement gap—the very opposite of the outcome we seek. This eventuality could come to pass if we do not take steps to reverse the patterns that led to the gap in the first place.

I argue that, if we wish to close the literacy achievement gap, we must take seriously the notion of building on the strengths that students of diverse cultural and linguistic backgrounds bring with them from the home—Key to Success #3. This is in contrast to the existing pattern, found in many schools, of teaching students according to conventional methods, based on mainstream assumptions that do not apply to many students of diverse backgrounds. As indicated in Chapter 2, I consider culturally responsive instruction to be one of the seven elements that must be considered in efforts to close the gap.

I wrote in Chapter 1 about conducting my research on culturally responsive instruction in classrooms in which the majority of students were of Native Hawaiian ancestry. Other early studies of culturally responsive instruction were similarly conducted in settings in which all or many of the students were from the same cultural background. Inadvertently, these studies led some educators to infer that culturally responsive instruction required a strict match between instructional practices and students' cultural backgrounds. These educators concluded that it was impractical to attempt to implement culturally responsive instruction in classrooms where students came from many different cultures, as is often the case in schools in urban districts.

I wrote this chapter specifically to address misconceptions about the need for a strict matching and to offer a formulation of culturally responsive instruction appropriate for multiethnic, multilingual settings. This formulation is based on the notion of a diverse worldview shared by members of many nonmainstream cultural groups. This chapter includes a discussion of the knottiest issues surrounding culturally responsive instruction: (1) moving beyond matching or the duplication of home settings to an understanding of hybridity, (2) holding to general principles of good teaching while accepting the need for differing instantiations, and (3) recognizing that teachers do not have to come from the same background as their students to apply culturally responsive instruction effectively.

What I would like you to take from this chapter is that culturally responsive instruction, Key to Success #3, is an approach that can and should be tried in schools serving high proportions of students of diverse cultural and linguistic backgrounds. As I implied earlier, I do not see culturally responsive instruction as a panacea. It cannot be our only response to the literacy achievement gap because—as indicated in Chapter 2—research conducted from a social constructivist perspective suggests that there are at least six other elements that must be considered. This is consistent with Key to Success #1, the idea that the gap is complexly determined. However, given the diversity of students' backgrounds, especially in urban districts, the time has come for educators to make every effort to understand a diverse worldview and to teach students in culturally responsive ways.

RISING STANDARDS FOR LITERACY

To set the context for this discussion of culturally responsive instruction, I begin by considering the state of literacy in developed nations such as Singapore and the United States. These nations have experienced rising standards for literacy with an acceleration in this trend over the past 100 years. Historical research in the United States demonstrates this dramatic rise (Kaestle, Damon-Moore, Stedman, Tinsley, & Trollinger, 1991).

In colonial America individuals were considered literate if they could sign their names. Today, however, signature literacy is considered an unacceptably low level of literacy even for 5-year-olds. In the second half of the 1800s a literate American was one who could declaim with expression a familiar passage that had been read many times before. Today we regard such oral reading with expression as an inadequate demonstration of literacy because it ignores the reader's comprehension of the text. In 1900, a time of massive immigration to the United States from southern and eastern Europe, the average American had a Grade 3 education—a level of literacy roughly equivalent to that of an 8-year-old today. In 1940, on the eve of World War II, the average American had a Grade 8 education. Standards for literacy rose rapidly in the second half of the twentieth century, and at present the expected level of literacy in the United States is considered to be at Grade 12. At this level students are expected to comprehend informational texts, such as primary and secondary historical texts, and to synthesize ideas from these different sources.

Note that standards for literacy have only moved in one direction—up. I believe it is reasonable to assume that standards for literacy will continue to rise and that students now in schools will be expected to meet even higher standards of literacy than in the past. An indication of this continued rise in the United States is the increased emphasis in large-scale reading assessments on constructed responses in which students must demonstrate their comprehension by presenting an interpretation and justifying it with evidence from the text (National Assessment of Educational Progress, 2010). Another indication is found in arguments that the definition of literacy should be expanded beyond print to encompass visual literacy, including the strategies needed to interpret multimedia presentations such as movies and websites (e.g., Lemke, 2006).

Why are standards rising? According to political observers such as Friedman (2000), the answer is globalization. Just as the agrarian economy gave way to the industrial economy, the industrial economy is losing ground to the knowledge and service economy. Friedman predicted that, in the world of the future, 93% of workers will be employed in knowledge and service fields, such as education, financial services, and tourism. Only 5% of workers will be employed in manufacturing, and only 2% in agriculture. As business leaders in the United States and Singapore realized over a decade ago, a nation that wants to maintain a vibrant economy in the era of globalization must educate its workers to outthink workers in other parts of the world.

I am not suggesting that the only purpose for literacy education and schooling is to produce workers for the global economy. In my opinion, literacy for the purposes of citizenship and personal fulfillment are equally, if not more, important. As educators, however, we must recognize that rising literacy standards attributable to globalization are part of macroeconomic trends that are highly unlikely to change in the foreseeable future. We must be aware of preparing the students in our classrooms today for the world of the future and the likelihood that they will need to be skilled at using advanced forms of literacy, such as higher-level thinking with text, to find success in the knowledge and service economy.

To provide a concrete illustration of just how rapidly standards for literacy have risen, I present an overview of literacy across four generations of women in my own family. In Chapter 1, I discussed the life of my maternal grandmother, Hew Ngim Moi, who did not have the opportunity to attend school either in her home village in the New Territories or in Hawai'i and never became literate in either Chinese or English. My grandmother had a strong belief in education and made sure that all of her children, her daughters as well as sons, had the chance to go to school.

My mother, Mun Kyau Hew Au, born in 1924, is her youngest child. My mother was in her senior year at Maui High School when Pearl Harbor was bombed by the Japanese on December 7, 1941. My mother went on to the University of Hawai'i the following year and graduated 4 years later with a bachelor's degree. My parents met when they were both students at the university. My siblings and I all had the opportunity to receive both undergraduate and graduate degrees. My sister Susan Au Doyle, born in 1951, earned a master's degree in business administration.

The literacy of my niece Kaitlyn Doyle, born in 1989, provides a striking contrast to that of my grandmother. To give just one example, when she was in Grade 8, Kaitlyn wrote for a website called fanfiction.net. At the time she was a fan of an animé series called Gundam Wing. Fans of this and other series can publish original stories featuring their favorite characters on this website, and they can receive messages from those who read their stories. One day Kaitlyn was reading through stories on fanfiction.net when she came across a passage that sounded strangely familiar. As she read on, she discovered that several paragraphs from one of her stories had been plagiarized by another writer. Kaitlyn emailed the webmaster about the problem, and when she checked back the next day, the offending story had been removed.

As you can see, Kaitlyn's opportunities to become literate and the world in which she lives are strikingly different from those of my grandmother. Kaitlyn and her peers are adept at forms of literacy entirely unknown to previous generations. Clearly, Kaitlyn and her contemporaries must be educated as thinkers so that they will be able to find their way in the high-tech world that plays such a major role in their lives. Students must be able to engage in higher-level thinking with text not only on the printed page but in the multimedia world of computers and the Internet.

Along with many educators, I welcome the interest in higher-level thinking with text motivated by rising standards for literacy. After a lengthy period of being eclipsed by debates about phonics, comprehension has returned to prominence in discussions of reading in the United States. Educators are once again seeking information about the teaching of comprehension strategies such as determining important information, monitoring comprehension, and question-answer relationships (Dole, Duffy, Roehler, & Pearson, 1991; Raphael & Au, 2005). In my work with teachers, I often emphasize two aspects of comprehension and higher-level thinking with text: critical evaluation, including teaching students to judge the reliability of sources and soundness of reasoning; and synthesizing, or integrating ideas and information from a variety of sources.

STUDENTS OF DIVERSE BACKGROUNDS
AND THE LITERACY ACHIEVEMENT GAP

This background of rising standards for literacy forms the context for considering issues of equity affecting students of diverse backgrounds, as defined in Chapter 2. What conclusions can be drawn about schools' success in helping students of diverse backgrounds to meet higher standards for literacy? To address this question, I turn to results of the reading assessment of the National Assessment of Educational Progress (NAEP), popularly known as the Nation's Report Card. NAEP is the only large-scale, federally funded testing program in the United States. The NAEP reading assessment reflects the rising standards for literacy I have described. At Grade 8, 40% of student time is given to items requiring higher-level thinking with text, specifically, 17% to making reader-text connections and 23% to examining content and structure.

Figure 3.1 presents the 2009 NAEP reading assessment results for students in Grades 4, 8, and 12 (National Assessment of Educational Progress, 2010). Moving from left to right, the sets of bars show the achievement of White, Black, Hispanic, Asian/Pacific Island, and American Indian students. The results show a mean scale score for Black students at Grade 12

Figure 3.1. Average Scale Scores for White, Black, Hispanic, Asian/
   Pacific Islander, and American Indian Students, 2009 NAEP Reading
   Assessment

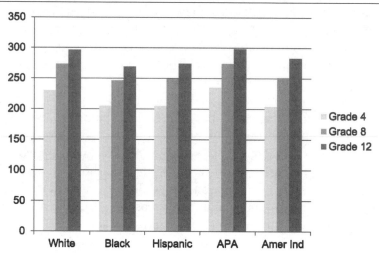

of 269, 4 points lower than the mean score of White students at Grade 8. The mean scale score for Hispanic students at Grade 12 is 274, the same as for Asian/Pacific Island students at Grade 8. Mean scores for American Indian students at Grade 12 are 13 points lower than for White students at this level. In short, NAEP results suggest that, by Grade 12, students of diverse backgrounds as a group have fallen about 4 years behind their peers in reading achievement.

The differences in achievement levels I have just described highlight the urgent need to address the literacy achievement gap. Rising standards for educational attainment confront us with the real danger that students of diverse backgrounds may be left farther behind their peers than ever before. In the United States recent NAEP results show that the literacy achievement gap has either remained the same or narrowed slightly (Rampey, Dion, & Donahue, 2009). Nevertheless, the gap remains unacceptably large.

Obviously, results obtained on tests such as the NAEP reflect only one kind of literacy, variously termed *autonomous, essayist,* or *mainstream* literacy (e.g., Street, 1995; for a discussion of essayist literacy, see Chapter 4). To foster the literacy of students of diverse backgrounds, educators must embrace the broader concept of literacy that Street terms *multiple literacies,* to include community uses of literacy associated with nondominant languages and nonmainstream cultural practices. Tse (2001) and other proponents of bilingual and multilingual education in the United States argue persuasively that the real issue is not the failure of immigrants to learn English. To the contrary, the evidence suggests that immigrants are motivated to learn English and tend to do so quite quickly. Instead, the real issue in the United States is preservation of students' many heritage languages and cultures.

Language loss can be swift and irreversible, and it can occur in a single generation. I illustrate this point by drawing again on my own family history. As mentioned in Chapter 1, my parents both spoke Chinese as their first language—my father, Cantonese, and my mother, Hakka. They switched gradually to speaking more and more English after entering school, and English became the dominant language for both of them. My father's first business was a grocery store in Honolulu's Chinatown, so he continued to speak "market Chinese" as an adult, and I recall as a youngster hearing my mother speak Hakka to my grandparents and to her siblings. However, my brothers and sister and I grew up speaking English and never learned to speak Chinese. There was no need to learn Chinese to communicate with the older generation, because my grandparents could all speak English. In my extended family, no one in my generation can speak Chinese. In the push toward Americanization, an important part of our heritage culture was lost.

In my judgment educators will want to have two goals when working with students of diverse backgrounds. The first goal is to help students acquire the knowledge, strategies, and skills that will enable them to meet higher standards for literacy and compete successfully for rewarding jobs in the global economy. The second goal is to allow students to reach higher standards through culturally responsive instruction or ways of teaching and learning consistent with the values of their heritage cultures.

EXPLANATIONS FOR THE GAP

In building the case for culturally responsive instruction, I want to pick up some threads from Chapter 2, where I discussed explanations for the literacy achievement gap. I established that the gap is complexly determined and may be attributed to the interaction of a number of different factors, such as poverty, that are difficult for educators to affect. Two particular explanations for the gap are relevant to this discussion of culturally responsive instruction. The first explanation is that the gap is, in part, attributable to the fact that students of diverse backgrounds have fewer opportunities than mainstream students to develop higher-level thinking with text. Research suggests that students of diverse backgrounds tend to receive a great deal of instruction emphasizing lower-level skills as opposed to higher-level thinking (Au, 2006; Darling-Hammond, 1995; Fitzgerald, 1995). The question educators must address is how we can give all students, and especially students of diverse backgrounds, access to instruction focused on higher-level thinking with text (Raphael & Au, 2005). Such instruction is clearly of vital importance in the era of globalization, when the challenge for educators is to bring all students to higher levels of literacy than ever before. I have argued that the emphasis on lower-level skills and rote learning so often seen in classrooms with students of diverse backgrounds is a consequence of low expectations for their academic achievement (Au, 2006).

The second explanation has to do with cultural incongruence, and this is the explanation emphasized in this chapter. The idea is that there is a disparity between typical schooling, or the way we usually "do school," and the literacy learning needs, preferences, and interests of students of diverse backgrounds. This disparity has the effect of making it difficult for students of diverse backgrounds to participate successfully in school literacy learning activities and therefore to attain high levels of literacy achievement in school.

Typical schooling fails to connect with the literacy learning needs and interests of students of diverse backgrounds in two ways. First, typical schooling is centered on content oriented to mainstream students and their perspectives. Many examples of the mainstream bias in curriculum content have been identified by researchers. In Hawai'i, for example, it is only in recent years that students have been taught about the Polynesian migration and the skills of the navigators who brought the ancestors of modern-day Native Hawaiians to the islands around 500–700 A.D. Previously, students in Hawai'i's schools were taught that the Hawaiian Islands were "discovered" by the British explorer James Cook in 1778.

Second, typical schooling is based on social processes oriented to mainstream students. These include an emphasis on whole-class (as opposed to small-group) teaching and use of the teacher initiation, student response, teacher evaluation—or initiation-response-evaluation (IRE)—pattern for structuring interaction (Mehan, 1979). In studies beginning in the 1970s researchers have demonstrated that use of the IRE pattern tends to pose a barrier to the successful participation in lessons of students of diverse backgrounds, including Native Americans (Philips, 1983) and Native Hawaiians (Au, 1980). The difficulty is that IRE requires students to demonstrate that they know the answer to the teacher's question by volunteering and speaking as individuals. The IRE reflects the value attached by the mainstream to competition and individual achievement, and these values are antithetical to those taught to many students of diverse backgrounds in the home. Native Hawaiian students, for example, are often raised to place a greater value on cooperation and working for the good of the extended family (Gallimore, Boggs, & Jordan, 1974).

CULTURALLY RESPONSIVE INSTRUCTION

Culturally responsive instruction is proposed as a solution to these disparities. Different labels have been used for this concept, including *culturally relevant pedagogy* (Ladson-Billings, 1995; Osborne, 1996), *culturally responsive teaching* (Gay, 2000), and *culturally congruent instruction* (Au & Kawakami, 1994). Rather than dwell on the nuances of differences among these terms, I highlight the assumptions shared by researchers who conduct studies in this area. One shared assumption is that the goal of culturally responsive instruction is to increase the school success of students of diverse backgrounds. Another assumption is that school success is to be achieved by building bridges between students' experiences at home and at school. The idea is to foster (or at the very least, to maintain) students' competence in the heritage culture and language. Finally, these researchers share the goal of promoting social justice through a focus on equality of educational outcomes and a celebration of diversity.

Culturally responsive instruction represents one of two theoretical paths for improving the literacy achievement of students of diverse backgrounds, as shown in Figure 3.2. Advocates of the first path, which I call the direct or assimilationist approach, believe that the school should immerse students of diverse backgrounds in mainstream content and interactional processes right from the outset. This is the dominant view of how education for students of diverse backgrounds should proceed. The second path shown in Figure 3.2 is what I call the indirect or pluralist approach; this is the path recommended by advocates of culturally responsive instruction. In the indirect path, schools first affirm and reinforce the cultural identity

Figure 3.2. Two Paths for Educating Students of Diverse Backgrounds

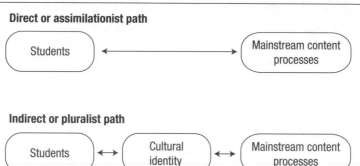

of students of diverse backgrounds. Working from this basis of cultural identity, educators then give students access to mainstream content and interactional processes.

The notion of culturally responsive instruction becomes complex because the concepts of culture and instruction are both complicated and subject to varying interpretations. Let me briefly deconstruct each of these concepts to clarify what I mean by culturally responsive instruction.

What makes culture such a slippery concept is that it has two different and seemingly conflicting dimensions. One dimension of culture centers on its stability and the other centers on its dynamism. Culture is simultaneously both stable and dynamic, and both dimensions must be addressed in efforts to improve the literacy achievement of students of diverse backgrounds (Au, 2006). The stable dimension refers to the fact that groups maintain cultural values across generations. For example, my grandmother grew up valuing education, although her family did not believe in sending girls to school, and this value was passed on to her while she was growing up in her home village in the New Territories. The dynamic dimension of culture refers to the fact that cultures may change as groups enter new settings and face new circumstances. In this case, my grandmother carried forward the value of education but extended it to include her daughters as well as her sons, because in Hawai'i girls had the opportunity to go to school.

Instruction, too, is a complex concept. From a constructivist perspective, I have interpreted instruction to consist of two parts (Au, 1993). First, the teacher must ensure that students become interested and involved in the learning activity. Second, once the students are engaged, the teacher must provide them with the support needed so that they can complete the activity successfully. A clear example of the application of this view of instruction is seen in the writers' workshop (Calkins, 1994). The teacher gets students engaged in writing from the heart by allowing them to choose topics important in their lives. Then the teacher provides students with minilessons on strategies and skills that enable them to succeed in the task of writing their personal narratives or memoirs. Minilessons may focus on strategies for planning, drafting, and revising; aspects of the author's craft, such as an interesting lead, voice, or repeated phrase, as shown in examples from children's literature; and skills such as spelling and punctuation.

In short, successful use of culturally responsive instruction requires some depth of understanding of both the concepts of culture and instruction. Often, an absence of this depth of understanding has led to misinterpretations of culturally responsive instruction. A common misinterpretation has been to treat culturally responsive instruction as if it required an exact matching or duplication of home environments in school (in other words, an overemphasis on the stable versus dynamic nature of culture). This misinterpretation was fostered in part by the nature of early studies of culturally responsive instruction that were conducted in classrooms in which most students were from the same ethnic or cultural group. This early research centered on differences in the patterning of face-to-face interaction, as exemplified in studies by Philips (1983).

In studies of the Warm Springs reservation in Oregon, Philips observed that Native American students preferred to avoid the teacher spotlight and did not volunteer to answer questions during classroom recitation. Philips connected the students' reluctance to the value placed on individual autonomy in this community. Students perceived classroom recitation to infringe on this value because the teacher, not the students, decided who should speak and at what moment. In this community, Philips noted, students decided for themselves when they had received adequate practice and were ready to begin participating in ceremonial events. Others did not impose this decision on them. Similar examples of cultural disparities and their correction through culturally responsive instruction were identified in my work with Native Hawaiian students (Au, 1980) discussed in Chapter 1; as well as by Piestrup (1973), Hollins (1982), and Foster (1989) in work with African American students; and McCollum (1989) in work with Puerto Rican students.

APPLICATION TO MULTIETHNIC CLASSROOMS

Although this work served to provide a firm empirical foundation for the concept of culturally responsive instruction, it also contributed to a misunderstanding on the part of some educators. These educators tended to assume that culturally responsive instruction required a duplication of home settings in school and an exact match between classroom interactional processes and students' backgrounds. This line of thinking led to the erroneous conclusion that culturally responsive instruction, although conceptually appealing, could only be used in classrooms in which students are homogeneous with respect to ethnicity and culture. As a result, it was mistakenly believed that the concept of culturally responsive instruction could not be applied to classrooms with students from a variety of cultural and linguistic backgrounds, a common situation in urban settings.

I conduct many classes and workshops with teachers, and this mistaken impression is reflected in one of the questions I am most frequently asked:

> I teach in an urban school and my students come from a dozen or more different cultural and linguistic backgrounds. Can teachers in a multiethnic setting like mine still use culturally responsive instruction?

The question of how the concept of culturally responsive instruction can be applied to multiethnic, multilingual classrooms is a vitally important one, because classrooms in large cities of the United States and other developed nations often include students from a dozen or more ethnic and linguistic backgrounds. Many teachers in urban settings doubt that they can use culturally responsive instruction because they assume that a matching of home environments is required. These teachers believe that they would have to gain an in-depth knowledge of their students' many different cultures to achieve a satisfactory degree of matching, and they doubt that they will have the time and opportunity to do so. Although I think it is important for teachers to understand their students' cultural backgrounds, I agree that gaining an in-depth knowledge of all the different cultures represented by students in an urban classroom can be a daunting and unrealistic task.

The approach I advocate avoids these difficulties. To address the situation of multiethnic classrooms, I recommend adopting a new perspective on culturally responsive instruction (Au, 2006). Instead of viewing culturally responsive instruction in terms of matching, this approach is based on considering contrasting worldviews, a Western or mainstream perspective versus a diverse or nonmainstream perspective. This approach is based on the seminal research of Spindler and Spindler (1990) on the American cultural dialogue and its transmission. These researchers identified a mainstream American worldview that contrasted sharply with the worldview of the Menominee, a Native American tribe.

Figure 3.3 shows my interpretation of these contrasting worldviews. I argue that many, though certainly not all, students of diverse backgrounds come to school with these or similar diverse values. It is not a matter of providing students of diverse backgrounds with classroom contexts exclusively based on one or the other of these worldviews. Rather, the approach is to incorporate both worldviews in the classroom. The mainstream perspective is valuable in preparing students to take advantage of opportunities offered by the larger society in the era of globalization. The diverse perspective is valuable in promoting learning by bridging the gap between home and school and by letting students work in ways valuable in settings outside of school (e.g., workplace settings typically require high levels of cooperation).

To understand the application of culturally responsive instruction to multiethnic classrooms, we must think of hybridity, not duplication, as foundational to the approach. An example of hybridity is seen in my research on talk-story-like participation structures in reading lessons taught to Native Hawaiian students (Au & Mason, 1981). A close analysis of these lessons shows that teachers shift among participation structures, sometimes following rules similar to those in community speech events

Figure 3.3. Contrasting Worldviews

Mainstream	Diverse
Individual effort	Working with others
Competition	Cooperation
Personal achievement	Well-being of the group
Success measured in material terms	Success measured in spiritual terms
Independence	Interdependence
People control nature	People live in harmony with nature

Source: Adapted from Spindler, G., & Spindler, L. (1990). *The American Cultural Dialogue and Its Transmission*. London: Falmer Press.

and sometimes following rules similar to those in conventional class-room recitation. The key community speech event in this case is talk story (Watson, 1975), in which speakers engage in co-narration and often over-lap one another's utterances. At times, teachers allowed several students to speak at once, and at other times they called on students to speak one at a time. In other words, these reading lessons did not duplicate talk story but were hybrid events in which teachers and students creatively combined elements of home and school culture.

I want to point out that such hybrid classroom events as talk-story-like reading lessons, occurring in the context of culturally responsive instruc-tion, have the intent of promoting academic achievement and not just of making students feel comfortable in school. These events serve to foster academic learning so that students of diverse backgrounds can achieve as well in school as their mainstream peers. In my studies of talk-story-like reading lessons, I assessed the effectiveness of lessons using proximal indi-ces of academic achievement, including the number of text ideas discussed and the number of logical inferences students made (Au & Mason, 1981). With Native Hawaiian students, these proximal indices were three to four times higher in talk-story-like reading lessons than in conventional lessons. Over time, it is reasonable to assume that the greater learning opportuni-ties offered by these lessons would contribute to significant improvements in achievement.

Also, culturally responsive instruction prevents students of diverse backgrounds from having to make the dreadful choice of leaving the home and peer culture in order to be successful in school. Fordham (1991) found that African American high school students from low-income backgrounds believed that they needed to "act White" and to separate themselves from home and peer influences to achieve success in school. Asking students of diverse backgrounds to make a choice between being true to their cultural identities and being successful in school puts them in an impossibly dif-ficult situation.

I do not think that students of diverse backgrounds should be con-fronted with such an either-or dilemma. Through culturally responsive instruction, I believe that educators can allow students to remain true to their cultural identities while attaining high levels of academic achieve-ment. Culturally responsive instruction allows students to attain academic success through classroom activities structured in ways that students find comfortable and understandable and that do not violate cultural values brought from the home.

DEFINING GOOD TEACHING

Another question I am frequently asked is this:

Isn't culturally responsive instruction just good teaching, and shouldn't good teaching be the same in every setting?

Gay (2000) addressed this point when she wrote about the widespread misconception that good teaching is universal and has nothing to do with the class, race, gender, ethnicity, or culture of students and teachers. This misconception is captured in the saying, "Good teachers anywhere are good teachers everywhere" (p. 22). Gay pointed out the logical flaw in this idea, namely that standards of goodness in teaching and learning are culturally determined and are not the same for all groups. For example, in some cultural groups a good teacher is considered to be one who gives instructions in a firm and direct manner and asks known-answer questions. In other cultural groups a good teacher is one who makes requests in an indirect manner and invites students to offer their opinions to open-ended questions.

Does this mean that it is impossible to define good teaching? Not at all. The way out of this conundrum is to define good teaching in terms of general principles whose instantiation may differ across settings. For example, a general principle of good teaching is that teachers should establish positive relationships with students. In mainstream classrooms this principle can be instantiated when the teacher praises individual students. In classrooms where students of diverse backgrounds may want to avoid being singled out by the teacher spotlight, this principle can be instantiated when the teacher gives positive feedback to a small group rather than individuals (e.g., "The students at Table 3 did good thinking by identifying the important information in the first paragraph").

Note that culturally responsive instruction does not limit students to participation structures they already use at home and within their communities. Limiting students' school experiences in this way would have the drawback of leaving them unprepared to interact successfully in school or other mainstream situations. For this reason, teachers must promote students' acculturation to unfamiliar or uncomfortable participation structures (such as IRE) important to school success. This acculturation to mainstream school participation structures can be promoted when the teacher establishes classroom routines and teaches students how to interact appropriately within these structures. The presence of consistent routines gives students the opportunity to learn the language and social skills expected of them. The advantage of routines is that students do not have to devote information processing capacity to figuring out how to behave appropriately and can instead direct available cognitive capacity to higher-level thinking and creative responses to text.

USING A VARIETY OF GROUPINGS

An important consideration in multiethnic classrooms is how teachers can incorporate both worldviews, the mainstream and diverse, especially to promote higher-level thinking with text. I believe that the starting point for incorporating both worldviews in the classroom is for the teacher to vary the form of grouping used during the school day. The goal of using a variety of groupings is to create a classroom in which every student can participate comfortably at least part of the time (Au, 2006). This goal cannot be achieved if all instruction is provided in only one type of grouping, such as lessons taught to the whole class. In addition to whole-class lessons, groupings should include the following:

- Teacher-led small groups
- Student-led small groups
- Work in pairs, such as partner reading and peer tutoring
- Individual or independent work

The writers' workshop (developed to teach the process approach to writing) and the readers' workshop (developed to provide literature-based instruction) are examples of approaches that incorporate a full range of groupings to promote students' higher-level thinking with text. The writers' workshop usually starts with a whole-class minilesson. The bulk of the workshop is devoted to writing time, which can include teacher-led small-group lessons, teacher and peer conferences, and individual writing. The writers' workshop often concludes with the Author's Chair (Graves & Hansen, 1983), a time for the whole class to come together to hear and respond to students' drafts or published pieces.

Book Club Plus, developed by Raphael and her colleagues (Raphael, Florio-Ruane, & George, 2001) is a particular form of the readers' workshop. Teachers who use this approach begin with a whole-class minilesson followed by individual or partner reading of novels. Students work individually to prepare written responses to the literature, then meet in book clubs (small groups of 4-6). In their book clubs, students share their written responses and guide their own discussions of novels, although the teacher monitors their conversations and may occasionally join a group. Another feature of Book Club Plus is teacher-led, small-group guided reading lessons focusing on text at students' instructional levels. Each session concludes with Community Share, a time when the teacher draws the whole class together for reflection and evaluation. In short, the writers' and readers' workshops follow routines that incorporate a variety of different groupings—ranging from whole class, to small group, to individual—and involve different participation structures.

Teachers will want to be aware of making explicit for students the rules for participation associated with each type of grouping. For example, teachers may want students to raise their hands before speaking during whole-class lessons, but turn control of turn taking over to students during small-group discussions. The purpose of having different rules for participation at different times of the school day should be explained so that they make sense for students. For example, the teacher might say:

> Now we're going to start Community Share. The rules for this time are that you must raise your hand if you want to say something. This is not a time when it's all right to call out an idea. I'm asking you to raise your hand first because there are 27 children in this room, and we won't be able to have a good class discussion if everyone starts talking at once.

The rules for appropriate participation need to be made explicit because students of diverse backgrounds may be learning to interact in ways previously unfamiliar to them. Teachers should set aside time at the end of the lesson or workshop for students to evaluate their own performance, both in terms of meeting academic demands and meeting expectations for participating appropriately.

The following question is another I am frequently asked: Wouldn't everything that you've recommended here also be beneficial for mainstream students? The answer is yes. The reason I emphasize the value of these practices for students of diverse backgrounds has been pointed out by Ladson-Billings (1994): These practices are rarely seen in classrooms with students of diverse backgrounds. It is essential to put new patterns in place for these students if we are ever to close the literacy achievement gap.

A final question that is frequently asked is the following: Can mainstream teachers who are outsiders to their students' cultures still implement culturally responsive instruction? Research findings consistently show that the answer to this question is yes. For example, in my research on talk-story-like reading lessons (Au & Mason, 1981), I found that teachers unfamiliar with Hawaiian culture could learn to teach lessons in this manner. Similarly, three of the eight successful teachers of African American students studied by Ladson-Billings (1994) were European Americans.

In the United States and other developed nations many students of diverse backgrounds are taught by teachers who come from mainstream backgrounds, and this situation in not likely to change in the near future. In the United States, for example, the proportion of teachers from culturally diverse backgrounds has actually decreased, even as the proportion of students of diverse backgrounds has increased (Au & Raphael, 2000). I believe it is important to make culturally responsive instruction a central part of teacher education, both during initial preparation and during ongoing professional development. Teachers need time to reflect on their own practice in terms of the two themes I have emphasized: culturally responsive instruction and higher-level thinking. I believe that the most effective programs of initial preparation and professional development are constructivist in nature and characterized by an essential parallel. In these programs, teachers engage in higher-level thinking and reflection so that they can better enable their students to do the same.

Through culturally responsive instruction and workshop approaches, we seek to transform classrooms into communities of learners. Similarly, through long-term, systemic change, we seek to affect the culture of the school and to transform schools into professional learning communities (see Chapter 7). Higher standards for literacy achievement do not merely entail raising the bar higher. Instead, higher standards should motivate us as educators to form professional learning communities with a shared vision about outcomes, while understanding that these outcomes may be reached by different paths.

CONCLUSION

Today's educators face rising standards for literacy as a consequence of the intense competition for economic standing fostered by globalization.

Rising standards for literacy lead to concerns about equity and whether educational systems are enabling all students to meet higher standards. The fact that we have not yet been successful in addressing issues of equity in education is shown by the existence of the literacy achievement gap. The question then arises of what educators can do to narrow or eliminate the gap, and I have recommended culturally responsive instruction as a possible solution. Culturally responsive instruction, Key to Success #3, captures the best of both worlds: It allows students to advance academically while participating in learning environments that do not require them to reject values—such as cooperation and working for the good of the group— brought from the home.

I have proposed a new formulation of culturally responsive instruction that moves away from a static notion of matching or duplicating home settings in school to a fluid notion based on hybridity and incorporating elements of a diverse worldview in classrooms. In the era of globalization the strength of a society depends on its ability to bring all of its citizens to higher levels of thinking, and culturally responsive instruction offers educators a powerful means of reaching this goal. Let us strive to bring all of our students to high levels of literacy by means that allow them to remain connected to their heritage cultures while stepping firmly into the future.

FOLLOW UP ACTIVITY

Discuss with colleagues the practical implications of implementing culturally responsive instruction in schools and classrooms. This discussion might include identifying barriers to change and determining how they might be overcome. Barriers might relate to educators' attitudes and reluctance to change, as well as to the practicalities of using a variety of groupings in classrooms.

Chapter 4

If Can, Can: Hawai'i Creole and Reading Achievement

I focus on issues of language in this chapter, developing the argument that speaking a home language other than Standard English is not a barrier to learning to read and write well in school. Why is it that students who speak a home language other than Standard English often do not achieve high levels of literacy in school? The answer, I believe, is an absence of adequate opportunities to master essayist literacy, including reading comprehension. Insufficient attention has been paid to Key to Success #2, which stresses the importance of higher-level thinking with text. Associated with this absence are low teacher expectations for students' performance and students' resistance to literacy learning in school. In keeping with Key to Success #4, whole school change, I discuss the importance of schools providing a coherent curriculum, focusing on essayist literacy for a period of 6 years or more, to enable students to develop the academic language proficiency necessary for long-term success in school and beyond.

For analytic purposes, it's often convenient to write about culture and language separately. As you can see, Chapter 3 was focused on culture, whereas this one is focused on language. However, I want to be sure to convey the idea that culture and language are intricately woven together and often inseparable. Issues of culture and language must be considered in tandem and educational solutions designed with both in mind, not just one or the other. Considerations of both language and culture are essential to Key to Success #3, culturally responsive instruction.

When we fail to make space in the classroom literacy curriculum for students' cultures and languages, we send students the unspoken message that the very things most central to their identity, the things they may hold most dear, do not count in school. Students' home cultures and languages should have a place and be valued in school settings. These resources brought by students from the home and community have value in and of themselves. They can also provide a bridge for teaching students essayist literacy.

I remember the day I learned that Hawai'i Creole (HC) was a language and not merely a form of broken English. This revelation came during a lecture given by one of my favorite professors, Betty Uehara. As Uehara discussed the *wen* past tense marker and other features of HC, I sat there in her language arts methods class wondering why I had never known of this perspective before. Having been born and raised in Hawai'i, I was astonished to think that I had grown up speaking a language so stigmatized that I had never believed it to be a language at all.

Twenty-five years later I would return as a professor to the University of Hawai'i, College of Education, to teach language arts courses myself. Because I found that most of my students were no better informed about HC than I had been, I often devoted a whole class to tackling the folk beliefs and misconceptions surrounding what most people in Hawai'i call "pidgin English." I would review the history of how HC had emerged as a lingua franca in Hawai'i during the 1890s, explain how HC had evolved by combining the syntax of the Hawaiian language with a lexicon drawn primarily from English, and draw comparisons to educational controversies surrounding African American Vernacular English (AAVE), such as the Ann Arbor case (Labov, 1982).

It was fascinating to watch students' faces as they digested this information and to hear the questions they raised. The reaction of most local students paralleled my own reaction so many years earlier: "Why didn't anyone tell me this before?" One student, a retired military officer who had returned to the university in order to become a teacher, asked several pointed questions, frowned, and was obviously struggling with the issues. After class he came up to me and extended his hand. "Thank you for the information you shared today," he said. "I had no idea, I just had no idea."

I do not believe that HC needs to be taught in the classroom as the basis for promoting reading achievement. Parents in Native Hawaiian communities have always indicated to me that they send their children to school to learn what they cannot easily teach them at home, including the kind of proficiency in American English that enables success in the larger society. Many of these parents would adamantly oppose attempts to teach students to read through HC texts, just as parents in African American communities opposed the use of "dialect readers," or texts for the teaching of reading written in AAVE (Rickford & Rickford, 1995). In African American communities, parents' opposition centered on concerns that their children would receive an inferior curriculum, with fewer learning opportunities than students in other schools to reach high levels of achievement in the reading of American English. I think these are legitimate concerns.

On one hand, I believe that American English, the language of power in the United States and thus in Hawai'i, is the language that must be emphasized if students are to learn to read well in school, in ways recognized by the larger society. On the other hand, I believe that rejecting students' home language is tantamount to rejecting the students themselves, as suggested by both research (Au, 2006) and personal experience. Therefore, even as American English must be the focus of instruction, students' home languages, including HC, must be acknowledged and treated with dignity and respect.

In this chapter, I review what I have come to understand about HC and its relationship to learning to read. This chapter is organized around four topics: (1) language, literacy, and power in Hawai'i; (2) HC and literacy learning; (3) resistance to learning literacy in school; and (4) sustained school change to improve the literacy learning of students who speak HC as their primary language.

LANGUAGE, LITERACY, AND POWER IN HAWAI'I

Every multicultural society has a language of power, the language spoken by members of the dominant group or groups, as well as languages that lack power, because they are spoken by members of the subordinate group or groups. The ascension of one language over another has long been a source of controversy in Hawai'i, as it has in many parts of the world. If we follow the changing landscape of language use in Hawai'i, beginning with the arrivals of the British explorer James Cook in 1778 and the first party of Congregational missionaries from New England in 1820, we can trace how the Hawaiian language was deliberately replaced by English as the language of power (Au & Kaomea, 2009). The use of English literacy was central to colonization efforts, in which Native Hawaiians were positioned as inferior to European Americans through letters, government reports, newspaper articles, and the like.

Because teachers of English were few and far between, the missionaries determined that it would be impractical to begin the schooling of Native

Hawaiians in that language (e.g., Armstrong, 1858). Therefore, efforts to teach Native Hawaiians to read and write proceeded in two stages. First, beginning in the 1840s, thousands of Hawaiians gained literacy in the Hawaiian language through the common or government schools, staffed entirely by Native Hawaiian teachers. In 1880, as more English-speaking teachers were becoming available, the Board of Education began a determined effort to replace the common schools with government English schools. Through the systematic closing of the common schools, sometimes upon the retirement of elderly Native Hawaiian teachers, English replaced Hawaiian as the language of instruction. In 1895 H. S. Townsend, inspector-general of schools, wrote, "As predicted in the last report, the schools taught in the Hawaiian language are dead" with only three remaining, enrolling just 59 students (Townsend, 1895). The infamous law of 1896 passed by the provisional government, banning the use of Hawaiian in schools, appears to have been largely a symbolic gesture, as the linguistic battle had already been won.

History reminds us that efforts to educate students and provide them with literacy in the language of power are not necessarily beneficial or even benign (Willis, 2002). Schooling in the language of power, including literacy learning, may be tied to dominant group efforts to reinforce control over the society. Because of the present dominance of American English in Hawai'i, it is easy to forget that, through the 19th century, Hawaiian, not English, remained the most widely spoken language in these Islands. By the 1860s, Native Hawaiian writers were fighting to preserve the culture and political and social standing of their people, for example, through newspaper articles and petitions in the Hawaiian language (Au & Kaomea, 2009). Native Hawaiians were able to take ownership of literacy and resist colonization by appropriating literacy for their own purposes.

In the 19th century, the Hawaiian language had its place even in many non-Hawaiian families. As mentioned in Chapter 1, my great-grandfather, Chun Lin Hung, ran a rice mill in Hulē'ia, Kaua'i. He grew the rice on land leased from a prominent businessman named George N. Wilcox. Because my great-grandfather could not speak English, and Wilcox could not speak Cantonese, they conversed in the one language they had in common—Hawaiian. The family surname was changed to Chun Ahana and then simply to Ahana, because that was the name by which my grandfather was known to his Native Hawaiian acquaintances. The very names of many of our local families reflect the widespread influence of the Hawaiian language in the 19th century.

Despite the banning of Hawaiian in schools, English did not replace Hawaiian as the lingua franca in plantation communities in the 1890s. Instead, the Hawai'i-born children of plantation workers grew up speaking HC to communicate with one another (Sato, 1985). As mentioned, while HC uses a largely English lexicon, its syntax is that of the Hawaiian language. For example, a speaker of HC might compliment a friend by saying "nice, your shoes" rather than "your shoes are nice." Because of its divergence from the American English spoken by members of the dominant groups in Hawai'i, HC was seen as a form of "broken English" in the popular press and in folk beliefs, rather than as a valid language in its own right. Through the 20th century, HC and its speakers were stigmatized, reinforcing their position as members of subordinate groups, just as the Hawaiian language and its native speakers had been stigmatized in earlier generations. A further irony in the 20th century was that the stigmatization of HC was at times carried out by Hawai'i-born legislators and educators who had themselves grown up as speakers of HC (Kua, 1999).

HC is one of the heritage languages of the people of the Hawaiian islands, along with Hawaiian, Ilokano, Japanese, Portuguese, and other languages. HC differs from other heritage languages in Hawai'i in that, as a lingua franca, it did not originate with any single ethnic group. HC is first and foremost a spoken language and does not have a standard orthography, although there is a steadily growing literature in HC, with writers such as Darrell Lum (1990), Lee Tonouchi (2001), and Lois-Ann Yamanaka (1996). In common with other heritage languages, HC connects its speakers to the history of their families and others who share a common cultural bond, in this case the Hawai'i plantation experience.

HC AND LEARNING TO READ

Speaking HC as a primary language does not prevent students from becoming excellent readers and writers of American English. The evidence for this assertion is seen in the many Hawai'i-born individuals who have grown up as speakers of HC and gone on to successful careers in a wide variety of fields, including those such as academics and the law, that require extensive use of American English and essayist literacy. All of these individuals, at some time in their lives, likely had the opportunity to learn essayist literacy, and to learn it well, perhaps at school or on the job. Essayist literacy, also known as *autonomous literacy* (Au, 2006; Street, 1995) is the kind of literacy valued in Western academic circles and evaluated on large-scale tests, the kind that gets students good grades in their high school English classes and allows them to write convincing essays when applying to college. In other words, it is the kind of literacy that gives an individual the appearance of being an intelligent and educated person, according to the cultural norms of the society's dominant groups.

As implied earlier, what gives a language prestige and power is neither its linguistic code nor its expressive potential but the socioeconomic status of its speakers. Gee (1990) reminds us that it is not the linguistic code alone we must master when we seek to learn a language well, but an entire discourse. His often quoted definition of a *discourse* is as follows: "A *Discourse* is a socially accepted association among ways of using language, of thinking, feeling, believing, valuing, and of acting, that can be used to identify oneself as a member of a socially meaningful group or 'social network', or to signal (that one is playing) a socially meaningful 'role'" (p. 143, italics in the original).

From the perspective of critical theory, one of the reasons it is important for the dominant groups in the society to elevate the prestige of their own language, and to denigrate the language of the subordinate groups, is to maintain their position of power. A command of the language of power—mastery of the discourse, in Gee's terms, and not just the linguistic code—is often a prerequisite for entry into the elite circles that control the society's major institutions, such as business, government, and education. In other words, to advance in society, individuals must usually speak, write, and otherwise present themselves in ways that signal their identity as dominant group members and their familiarity with the culture of power. A discourse allows those within its purview to distinguish between "us" and "them." In keeping with a critical analysis, it follows that access to the language of power must necessarily be carefully controlled, readily available to children of the dominant groups yet difficult to obtain for children of the subordinate groups. Schooling in the language of power is treated as a precious resource, to be carefully distributed for the benefit of the few.

In the history of Hawai'i a well known example of the rationing of schooling in the language of power and essayist literacy is seen in the English standard schools, which had their beginnings in 1920. These schools were opened at the behest of European American parents who wanted their children educated in an American English environment, apart from the HC-speaking children of working-class families. These schools provided an attractive option for parents unable or unwilling to pay for a private school education. Ostensibly, public schools with this designation were to provide the opportunity for any qualified students to receive a rigorous education. In practice, students were admitted on the basis of their proficiency in American English, at a time in Hawai'i's history when most students grew up speaking HC as their first language. Thus, especially in the early years, students from European American families could pass the test of English proficiency required for admission, while others could not.

Inequality in reading achievement serves as just one sign of how effectively the channeling of access to the language of power and essayist literacy continues to work in the United States. In Chapter 3 I described in detail the reading test results on the National Assessment of Educational Progress (NAEP), which show that by Grade 12, African American students as a group have fallen about 4 years behind White students as a group (National Assessment of Educational Progress, 2010). I have not seen a comparable analysis of results by ethnic groups on the Hawai'i state reading tests, introduced in 2001-02, but past standardized reading test results reported in the Native Hawaiian Educational Assessment Program (NHEAP; Kamehameha Schools Office of Program Evaluation and Planning, 1993) showed a layering of scores on standardized reading tests, with European American and Japanese American students scoring above the national average and students of Native Hawaiian and Filipino American ancestry scoring below the national average.

These results suggest that access to essayist literacy is selectively distributed in my state, just as it is in the rest of the nation. My view is that it is the lack of opportunity to learn essayist literacy well, rather than the fact that they speak HC as a primary language, that accounts for some Hawai'i-born students' poor showing on tests of reading achievement.

Anecdotal evidence to support this view appeared in an article in the Honolulu Advertiser with the following lead: "Fifty years after graduating from Maui's only English-standard school, half of the members of Kaunoa School's class of 1957 returned to the site of their former campus this month to install a commemorative plaque" (Wilson, 2007). This class, the last to complete Grade 8 at Kaunoa, included Maui Mayor Charmaine Tavares; Shirley Kodani Cavanaugh, a retired Air Force lieutenant colonel; Gaylord Kubota, director of the Alexander and Baldwin Sugar Museum; and Warren Shibuya, a former instructor in aerospace management at the University of Hawai'i. In their comments, the graduates expressed their appreciation for the education they had received at Kaunoa. Cavanaugh noted that, while they learned at school to communicate well in American English, the students still spoke "pidgin" (HC) when they went home and had the ability to switch between the two codes.

One of the lessons to be learned from these graduates' experience at Kaunoa is that it was perfectly possible for public schools in Hawai'i to teach students who grow up speaking HC to master essayist literacy and speak American English well. One of the features distinguishing the English standard schools appears to be that teachers held high expectations for their students and, as a result, may have taught following a more academically rigorous curriculum than in other public schools. Research continues to verify the hypothesis of the self-fulfilling prophecy, demonstrating the role of teachers' perceptions of students. These perceptions predict changes in student achievement beyond differences accounted for by students' prior achievement and motivation (Jussim & Eccles, 1992).

In common with all members of a society, educators are subject to the influence of dominant group discourse, and this discourse can be used to keep those who do not speak the language of power in a position of inferiority (e.g., Au & Kaomea, 2009). Such is the case, for example, when an Associated Press article refers to "pidgin English" as "an amalgamation of Hawaiian and foreign words spoken with a cadence that is almost impenetrable to the malihini (newcomer)" (Dunford, 1999). It is not surprising, then, that listeners judge a speaker of American English as superior to a speaker of HC, even when the two are presenting the same ideas (Ohama, Gotay, Pagano, Boles, & Craven, 1999). Consciously or subconsciously, many still seem to assume that sound reasoning can only be expressed in the language of power, a myth debunked by sociolinguistic research dating from the 1970s. Labov's (1973) classic research on the logic of nonstandard English, specifically AAVE, included a striking transcript of skillfully constructed, spontaneous arguments about the existence and nature of God, proposed by Larry, a young African American from the inner city. Labov observed that Larry's arguments, stated entirely in AAVE, were entirely understandable and convincing, leaving no doubt that he could use the English language effectively for a wide range of purposes.

In analyzing the Black-White test score gap, Ferguson (2003) argued that teachers' perceptions, expectations, and behaviors interact with students' beliefs, behaviors, and work habits to perpetuate educational inequities. A parallel set of circumstances may well be affecting many HC-speaking students, particularly those attending schools in low-income communities. While I do not believe that teacher perceptions are the only reason for below-average reading achievement results, many Hawai'i educators will have witnessed the phenomenon of low teacher expectations at work. Low teacher expectations for students' performance have been identified as a key issue in accreditation and other external evaluation reports for more than one high school in my state. I saw the phenomenon of low expectations several years ago, when I was working with a team of teacher leaders from a rural high school in which the vast majority of students spoke HC as their primary language. The task I had presented to the team was to draft a vision statement of the excellent writer who graduated from their school, a task that has not posed a problem to any group of teachers before or since. This particular team of teachers insisted that they could not develop a vision statement describing the excellent writer who graduated from their school. The reason, they asserted, was that their school did not have any students who could become excellent writers.

A vicious cycle may be at work in some schools with high numbers of students who speak HC as their primary language. Some teachers may hold low expectations for students' academic performance, believing that students are poor language users because they speak a form of "broken English." Low expectations may contribute to what has bluntly been termed a "dumbing down" of the curriculum, in which students may not have the opportunity to learn essayist literacy well. Under these circumstances it would not be surprising to see students, as a group, failing to develop reading comprehension and critical analysis abilities, as well as performing below state targets or national norms on large-scale tests of reading achievement. Schools where teachers hold low expectations for students tend to move toward packaged programs that emphasize lower-level, basic reading skills, thus depriving students of lessons focusing on reading comprehension, reasoning with text, and the literary content (classic and contemporary literature) that contribute to proficiency in essayist literacy.

Barbara Taylor and her colleagues have verified in study after study that an emphasis on phonics is positively related to reading achievement in first grade, but negatively related to achievement in second and third grade (Taylor, Pearson, Clark, & Walpole, 2000; Taylor, Pearson, Peterson, & Rodriguez, 2003, 2005). At all grades studied, teachers' use of higher-level questioning contributes significantly to stronger reading achievement. These findings resonate with those of research conducted at KEEP, as indicated in Chapter 1 (Tharp, 1982). Students' difficulties may be compounded when educators think the solution to poor reading test scores is to extend lower-level skill instruction to higher and higher grades. Amazingly, I have even heard intensive phonics instruction proposed as a solution for the reading difficulties of high school students in Hawai'i. While I am a proponent of phonics instruction (Au, 2006; see Chapter 6), I am convinced by the research of Taylor and others that phonics instruction should be systematically taught and completed in the early primary grades, leaving time for teachers to address the much more challenging task of promoting reading comprehension.

RESISTANCE TO LITERACY LEARNING IN SCHOOL

I turn now to issues of students' resistance to literacy learning in school (addressed also in Chapter 5), another important way that HC is related to reading achievement. Proponents of resistance theory (e.g., Erickson, 1993) contend that subordinate group students (which would include many students who speak HC as their primary language) consciously and subconsciously oppose school actions that threaten their cultural identities. For example, students may show resistance by ignoring the teacher, refusing to participate, turning in incomplete assignments, or acting out in class, and fail to make strong academic progress as a result. Student resistance can develop quickly if teachers signal their low regard for students' culture (Larson & Irvine, 1999) or cast aspersions upon their primary language (Erickson, 1993; Piestrup, 1973).

D'Amato (1993) points out that all children resist school to some extent. However, resistance does not persist in the case of dominant group students, who understand the importance of cooperating with teachers and doing well in school and know the relationship between schooling and life opportunities: complete high school, graduate from college, and qualify for a high-paying job. For many students from affluent families, these connections are reinforced by family history. The situation is different for subordinate group students, with the connections typically being much weaker. For example, in African American communities, discrimination may prevent even a well-educated, highly qualified individual from obtaining a desirable job (Ogbu, 1981).

D'Amato's (1988) research shows that resistance can be seen even in early elementary grades classrooms. He suggests that teachers do not hold the cards in classrooms where their students are unfamiliar with the long-term rewards of schooling. This situation arises because students are not concerned about the consequences of offending teachers or doing poorly in school. D'Amato argues that teachers must win students over by making school a rewarding and enjoyable experience in an immediate sense. One means of capturing students' interest is through culturally responsive instruction, instruction that builds on the strengths that students bring from the home, including their cultural and linguistic knowledge (see Chapter 3). My research at KEEP showed that interactive discussions of literature, using talk-story-like participation structures, kept students highly engaged in learning to read (Au & Mason, 1981). We found at KEEP that Native Hawaiian students achieved at higher levels in learning to read when their teachers took the approach of making lessons personally meaningful to them. Teachers could accomplish this by making connections between students' background experiences and the theme of the story (Au, 1992) and by emphasizing reading comprehension or meaning making with text and not just word identification skills (Tharp, 1982).

A newer option, not available in the 1980s, is to increase students' motivation to read through the use of local literature reflecting experiences of growing up in Hawai'i. These works range all the way from concept books for preschool and kindergarten, such as *Whose Slippers Are These?* (Kahalewai, 2005) to teen novels such as *The Tattoo* (McKinney, 2007). Works written in HC might be included in the curriculum, along with the canonical works of literature typically taught in middle and high schools, as long as teachers and the community feel comfortable with this decision.

Students' ownership of literacy may be defined as their valuing reading and writing as part of their lives and using literacy for purposes they set for themselves (see Chapter 5). Ownership of literacy must be foundational to attempts to improve reading achievement in schools serving high numbers of students who speak HC as their primary language, and ownership may be improved if students read works of literature they find meaningful.

Teachers can and should take steps to make ownership of literacy the overarching goal of classroom reading instruction. However, while ownership plays an important role, it is a necessary but not sufficient condition for improving reading achievement in classrooms with students who are growing up outside the culture of power, such as many who grow up speaking HC as their primary language. If young students have the motivation to read, this is an important first step that will boost their learning of word identification skills. However, it will not automatically improve their performance in reading comprehension (Au, 1994). To improve students' comprehension, instruction specifically targeting strategies of reading comprehension must be provided. Just because students know all the words in a text does not mean that they will automatically comprehend it. Rather, research shows that instruction in comprehension is required if students' ability to derive meaning from text is to improve (Anderson, Mason, & Shirey, 1984). In addition, research indicates which comprehension strategies are most valuable to teach students (Dole et al., 1991; Raphael, Highfield, & Au, 2006).

Instruction focused on higher-level thinking with text can be highly motivating to students and thus serve an important function in overcoming students' resistance to schooling. My colleague Alice Kawakami, a former KEEP teacher who became a professor in the College of Education at the University of Hawai'i, once described how she attempted during reading comprehension discussions to make her third-grade students "feel smart." Indeed, those who have observed and studied reading comprehension lessons taught by KEEP teachers agree that these discussions cause elementary students to engage with text ideas as deeply and actively as graduate students in a seminar. Students who come away from a lesson feeling smart are likely to think of school as a worthwhile place to be, because they have engaged with interesting ideas, argued and justified their points of view, and had their teacher confirm their potential as good thinkers.

SUSTAINED SCHOOL CHANGE

All students can benefit from rigorous instruction in reading comprehension to prepare them to use essayist literacy in the ways demanded by the higher academic standards now in place in Hawai'i and across the rest of the country. However, such rigorous instruction is particularly important to the academic futures of students who speak HC as their primary language and grow up outside the culture of power. These students will be largely dependent on school for access to dominant group discourse and essayist literacy. Furthermore, research suggests that it will take 6 years or more for students who speak HC as a primary language to gain the proficiency in American English foundational for essayist literacy. This is why school change efforts that focus only on grades K–3 or only on beginning reading frequently do not show significant effects on students' long-term achievement. While certain early interventions do have a positive effect on children' reading in the primary grades, these interventions show diminishing effects and do not provide a sufficient basis for success with the more demanding reading tasks at the third and fourth grades and above (Hiebert & Taylor, 2000).

It is important to understand why a period of 6 years or more of well-coordinated, rigorous instruction may well be required to make a difference in the overall reading achievement of many HC-speaking students. Let us begin by referring to Cummins's (2003) distinction between *basic interpersonal communication skills* (BICS) and *cognitive academic language proficiency* (CALP). Teachers are often amazed that children who enter the classroom speaking Spanish or another language are, within months, communicating with other children in English. Part of the reason for this rapid learning is undoubtedly the need and desire to join peer groups and participate in activities on the playground and in other settings and to meet the needs of everyday life, such as shopping for groceries. The rapid learning of BICS is supported by the fact that interactions are embedded in meaningful contexts, with referents right at hand.

Due to television as well as home and community experiences, some students who speak HC as a primary language may come to school with BICS in American English. We had a favorite videotape at KEEP that captured the language proficiency of one of our first-grade students from Kalihi. (Pseudonyms have been used for the student and teacher in this anecdote.) The tape showed Branden working on a seatwork assignment while at the same time speaking HC to threaten another boy at his table, waving his fist in front of his peer's face and declaring that they would be fighting at recess. As the teacher, newly arrived from the continental United States, approached his table, Branden looked up and asked sweetly, in clearly enunciated American English, "Miss Moran, may I sharpen my pencil?" When the teacher nodded, Branden left the table, returning after a moment to resume his threatening in HC.

As this anecdote implies, many HC-speaking students can easily switch between HC and American English, suggesting that they have BICS in American English and could advance to CALP and attain proficiency in essayist literacy. However, two caveats must be considered. The first, discussed earlier, is the prediction of resistance theory that subordinate group students may decide that they do not want to attain essayist literacy. Any teacher who has taught in a Title I (low-income) school in Hawai'i has struggled to reach any number of students with such an attitude. Ogbu (1993) described how subordinate group students might well show resistance because of the need to maintain their cultural identities in the face of what they perceive to be an unfamiliar and threatening school environment, one that does not seem to value their talents, language, or culture. Students might choose to express themselves only in HC and not in American English as a means of maintaining their cultural identity and expressing solidarity with peers.

Second, it should be noted that CALP and essayist literacy are not easy targets, making 6 years a conservative estimate of the amount of instructional time required (Collier, 1989). For example, consider the cognitive demands of a typical fourth-grade science lesson about the origin of the Hawaiian islands. (I have observed several effective lessons along exactly these lines and know that the teachers considered their expectations to be perfectly reasonable for Hawai'i fourth graders.) During such a lesson the teacher will teach abstract concepts (plate tectonics) and use specialized vocabulary unlikely to be heard in everyday life (terms such as magma and caldera). Students will usually be unfamiliar with these concepts and terms, unless they have already visited an area such as Volcanoes National Park, and the teacher will need to refer to models, diagrams, and photographs to get these points across. At the end of the lesson, the teacher will ask students to read a short newspaper article on the island of Lō'ihi, growing underwater near the island of Hawai'i (southernmost and youngest in the Hawaiian chain), and write a summary of the article, making connections to ideas covered in the lesson. Obviously, to perform well in the classroom even in elementary school, students need CALP and essayist literacy; BICS are insufficient for the learning of the academic content routinely being taught in elementary schools, as well as middle and high schools.

Fortunately, there is a tremendous amount of research on how students who grow up speaking HC or other nonmainstream varieties of English can be taught to become excellent readers and writers, as judged by the standards of essayist literacy (Au, 1993, 2006; Guthrie et al., 1996; Morrow, 1992; Raphael & Au, 2005). Unfortunately, my research and experience in schools point to the distinct possibility that many HC-speaking students, particularly in schools in low-income communities, usually do not receive enough high-quality, coordinated instruction over the period of time—6 years or more—required for them to gain a solid grasp of CALP in American English and of essayist literacy. Unlike students from affluent families, HC-speaking students from low-income families may have little contact with the discourse of the culture of power, at home or in community settings. Thus these students are highly dependent on school to gain familiarity with this discourse and to develop CALP.

Up to now I have discussed steps that teachers can take in classrooms. However, it is obviously important to consider the school and not just the actions of individual teachers, if the goal is to provide students with 6 years or more of effective, coordinated instruction to build proficiency in essayist literacy. To achieve this goal, teachers in a school must collaborate to build a staircase, or coherent, curriculum across the grades, as discussed in Chapter 7.

The approach my colleagues and I use to guide teachers through the process of creating a staircase curriculum is called the Standards-Based Change (SBC) Process (Au, Hirata, & Raphael, 2005; see Chapter 7). The SBC Process has been successfully used in some Hawai'i Title I schools with high proportions of students who speak HC as a primary language, including Kīpapa, Makakilo, and Helemano elementary schools. These three schools received awards from the Castle Foundation for increasing the number of students meeting and exceeding proficiency on the Grade 3 state reading test by 20% or more between 2003 and 2006. The SBC Process has also been effective in improving reading achievement in Chicago schools enrolling high proportions of students who speak either AAVE or Spanish as their primary language (Raphael, 2010).

Over time, this approach has come to center on the Seven Levels to Success, a developmental model that describes the stages of growth shown by schools successful in improving student achievement through the SBC Process (Raphael, Au, & Goldman, 2009). When a school reaches Level 6, scores on state reading tests rise and teachers have taken ownership of the change process. In short, the developmental model has given us a road map for school change that improves students' reading achievement. Teachers at schools working with the SBC Process are guided through a nine-step To Do Cycle (Au, Hirata, & Raphael, 2005; Au & Raphael, 2007). These nine components must be in place for a school to have a complete system for improving student achievement through standards. Teachers at public schools in Hawai'i and the rest of the country have been working with standards for about 2 decades. Thus every school is likely to have strengths, as well as weaknesses, in terms of the components on the To Do Cycle. We ask teachers to keep in place all the components they think are working well to foster student learning, and to use their time with the To Do Cycle to address any weaknesses.

Unlike most approaches to school improvement, the SBC Process is based on the premise that teachers at each school can and should create the school's own staircase curriculum in reading. The staircase curriculum is contrasted with the fragmented curriculum, which is the situation we have observed at all schools new to the SBC Process. The fragmented curriculum results because, although teachers at the various grade levels have good ideas for curriculum and instruction, they have not had sufficient time and guidance to coordinate their ideas across the grade levels.

One of the most common and insidious misconceptions we see in schools is the belief that purchasing a packaged reading program will automatically provide the school with a staircase or coherent curriculum. Research conducted in schools in Chicago showed that purchasing a packaged program did not lead to curriculum coherence because teachers could interpret and teach a program in many different ways (Newmann, Smith, Allensworth, & Bryk, 2001). Our research suggests that a staircase curriculum cannot be bought off the shelf—it must be created through close collaboration within and across grade levels and departments. We guide teachers at each school in the SBC Process through the equivalent of four professional development courses to help them build the staircase curriculum (Au, Raphael, & Mooney, 2008b). In elementary schools, a staircase curriculum must be built for every major content area: reading, writing, math, science, and social studies. It often takes a school 2 to 3 years to learn the SBC Process and complete work in the first content area. My colleagues and I describe the SBC Process as the "sure and steady fix." As research shows, there is no such thing as a "quick fix" (Allington & Walmsley, 1995), despite the claims of promoters of some packaged programs.

We can empathize with the difficulties faced by superintendents, principals, and other administrators responsible for leading schools with a history of low reading test scores. These leaders are under tremendous pressure to show marked improvement in results. It is all too tempting under these circumstances to look for ready-made external solutions for improving test results. Our experience has been that external solutions, such as packaged programs, often do not yield the kinds of lasting improvement necessary to provide HC-speaking students in low-income communities with excellent opportunities to gain essayist literacy. One of the reasons is variability in teachers' interpretations and ways of implementing the external program. Another reason is gaps in the external program in relationship to state standards. Still another reason is that the external program does not cover all the curriculum areas students need. For example, teachers using basal reading programs typically see weaknesses in provisions for reading comprehension strategy instruction.

Nevertheless, the fatal flaw in the implementation of external programs may lie less in their design than in the fact that teachers do not feel ownership over them. When their schools rely on external programs, teachers may tend to attribute students' progress (or lack of progress) to the program rather than to their own efforts. Yet, as the saying goes, programs don't teach—teachers teach. In SBC Process schools successful in improving student achievement, teachers take ownership of change efforts and feel a sense of efficacy and personal responsibility for their students' achievement. At successful schools administrators trust teachers to make good decisions within the framework of the SBC Process, and the whole school pulls together as a professional learning community to create and implement a staircase curriculum, covering all grades, to promote student achievement. Teachers believe that their students can and will become excellent readers, and teachers provide instruction focused on higher-level thinking as well as basic skills. Students sense that their language and culture are respected by teachers and find lessons engaging and challenging. Rather than showing resistance, students willingly cooperate with teachers to learn essayist literacy.

As students move through the grades and up the staircase curriculum, they receive instruction that builds on what they learned the year before. Due to the well-coordinated instruction fostered by the staircase curriculum, cohorts of students begin to enter each successive grade at higher levels of achievement than did earlier cohorts. In schools with a low rate of student transiency, this effect is particularly noticeable in Grade 4 and above. When teachers notice students' higher entering achievement levels, they know that they can move students farther ahead as readers, and they create more ambitious end-of-year grade-level benchmarks. The staircase curriculum exerts its positive effect through teachers' steadily rising expectations for students' learning, which lead to improved results on large-scale achievement tests (Au, Raphael, & Mooney, 2008a).

CONCLUSION

In common with most local people of my generation who were born and raised in Hawai'i, I did not grow up valuing HC. I spoke it, I heard others speak it, and I knew that the use of "pidgin" was considered inappropriate in certain settings, but I did not give these matters much thought. Today, I can appreciate my good fortune in having grown up speaking HC and having the continued opportunity to use the language. Being a speaker of HC is a treasured marker of local identity, a connection to my family's plantation roots.

As recently as 1999 local politicians—notably, former governor Ben Cayetano—were sometimes criticized in the newspapers for "lapsing" into HC. Rest assured that when skillful local politicians such as Cayetano incorporate HC in their public pronouncements, they are doing so intentionally, for rhetorical effect. Prosodic and phonological shifts in particular, toward HC and back again toward American English, can be observed in the speech of many successful Hawai'i-born individuals. Those with an ear for the cadences of local speech enjoy the banter and linguistic feats of radio personalities such as Sam Kapu, who mix HC and American English with wit and skill. We do not need to teach HC in the classroom, but we do need to respect and appreciate it as one of the heritage languages of the Hawaiian islands, and this respect needs to be conveyed to students who speak HC as their primary language.

I have shown in this chapter that, since Western contact, Hawai'i has been a multilingual environment, with language serving to separate the dominant groups from the subordinate groups, as is typical in ethnically and culturally diverse societies. English became the language of power and was effectively used to place the Hawaiian language and its speakers, and then HC and its speakers, in subordinate positions. Historically, HC-speaking students in low-income communities have had limited access to CALP in American English and essayist literacy, as required to perform well on large-scale tests of reading achievement. The problem of increasing students' access is not a simple one, with students' resistance to school literacy learning posing a potential problem. Resistance by students may develop when their home language and culture are not respected in school, when they sense that teachers have low expectations for their academic learning, when instruction overemphasizes basic skills to the exclusion of higher-level thinking, and when lessons cease to be engaging and meaningful.

I proposed use of the SBC Process to guide schools' development of staircase curricula as an effective approach for improving the reading achievement of students who speak HC as a primary language. A staircase curriculum is necessary to provide students with the coordinated, high-quality instruction they need, across a period of 6 years or more, to gain proficiency in essayist literacy. As noted earlier and discussed in detail in Chapter 7, this approach to schoolwide change is a sure and steady fix, not a quick one, that has worked to raise reading achievement in schools in Hawai'i and Chicago.

A student in one of my undergraduate courses came to class one day wearing a T-shirt with the following HC phrases:

If can, can. If no can, no can.

Translation: "If I can possibly do it, I will. If I find that it can't be done, don't expect anything." We must believe, beyond the shadow of a doubt, that students who speak HC and other nonmainstream varieties of English as their primary language can and will become excellent readers. To be successful, we must rely on sound professional development to prepare teachers with the knowledge and confidence they need to hold high expectations, build their school's staircase curriculum, and teach essayist literacy well. If can, can.

FOLLOW-UP ACTIVITY

Trace the languages spoken in the various generations of your own family. These languages might include regional dialects and nonmainstream varieties of English, as well as other languages such as Spanish or Cantonese. Consider in your reflection the circumstances that influenced preferences for one language or another in different generations of your family. Did these circumstances affect access to instruction in essayist literacy? Discuss your reflections with the members of your group. What practical implications do you see for the literacy instruction of English language learners?

Chapter 5

Ownership, Literacy Achievement, and Students of Diverse Cultural Backgrounds

In this chapter I provide a summary of research conducted during the last years of the Kamehameha Elementary Education Program (KEEP), the 24-year research and development effort aimed at improving the literacy achievement of Native Hawaiian students, a program that I mentioned in earlier chapters. I describe how a curriculum can be structured to address students' ownership of literacy as the overarching goal and provide classroom examples of teaching consistent with this curriculum. This type of constructivist or balanced literacy curriculum is discussed as well in Chapter 6.

At KEEP we found two approaches that proved highly effective with our students: the writers' workshop, based on the process approach to writing, and the readers' workshop, a form of literature-based instruction. I believe that one of the reasons these approaches worked so well is that they provide frameworks within which it is easy for teachers to introduce Key to Success #2, an emphasis on higher-level thinking with text, and Key to Success #3, culturally responsive instruction. I think the writers' workshop and readers' workshop could prove equally effective in other schools serving many students of diverse cultural and linguistic backgrounds.

Principals and other school leaders sometimes turn away from writers' and readers' workshops because they think their teachers lack the knowledge to implement workshop approaches successfully. It's true that the successful use of these approaches requires a high level of teacher expertise. But to my way of thinking, the answer is to begin right away to develop teachers' expertise with a well-planned, multiyear sequence of professional development. Taking shortcuts—for example, by adopting highly structured programs that appear to remove the need for teacher decision making—results in moving schools away from Keys to Success #1, 2, and 3.

This chapter includes more details about the research for which I am best known, namely culturally responsive instruction and talk-story-like participation structures. Drawing upon anthropological research, I explain how teachers' use of culturally responsive instruction can lead to improved student engagement and literacy achievement. One of the reasons culturally responsive instruction is so important is that students find it enjoyable and rewarding in an immediate sense. Culturally responsive instruction, such as lessons incorporating talk-story-like participation structures, can make learning interesting, engaging, and intellectually challenging for students.

One of my preservice students at the University of Hawai'i hailed from a rural community on one of the neighboring islands. As she was finishing her degree in education and preparing to return home, she came to speak to me. "I want to teach my students the process approach to writing," she said. "But what if I'm the only one in my school teaching that way? What will happen to the students when they move to the next grade?" I assured this student that I knew other teachers in her community who had been teaching the process approach to writing for years. But, I told her, suppose you *were* the only one—you must still go ahead and give your students the best literacy learning experiences you can. If you succeed in teaching them to write from the heart, you have given them something of value for the rest of their lives.

A VISIT TO A KEEP CLASSROOM

Now let's pay a visit to a KEEP classroom where the teacher is implementing the constructivist curriculum, featuring the writers' workshop. Pseudonyms have been used for the teacher and students.

Mrs. Nakamura, a second-grade teacher, had copied Nathan's report on sharks on chart paper for a minilesson on the qualities of effective writing. The report began:

> Hello, I'm Mr. Fernandez. I'm your leader to the undersea world of sharks. Today we will all follow the great white shark. Everybody put on your suits and tanks and goggles and fins.

Nathan had gotten the idea for writing his report as a guided tour from his classmate Moana, who had written a piece on the stars. In turn, Moana had been inspired by science books written by children's author Joanna Cole, in which students in Ms. Frizzle's class journeyed on a magic school bus.

Mrs. Nakamura pointed out Nathan's use of humor: "Sharks like meat and you are meat." His classmates noticed that he had chosen his phrases with care: "The part you have to worry about is. . . ." Nathan said he had borrowed this phrase from a videotape, *The Fox and the Hound*.

Like many of Mrs. Nakamura's students, Nathan is of Native Hawaiian ancestry, comes from a low-income family, and speaks Hawai'i Creole as a first language. Students with these background characteristics frequently achieve at low levels in school (Kamehameha Schools, 1993). However, at the time Nathan had completed his report, he and the other students in Mrs. Nakamura's class were viewing writing in surprisingly sophisticated ways. For example, Nathan had incorporated wording from a videotape viewed at home in his research report. He and other students knew how to draw upon ideas from children's literature and their classmates' writing. Entries in their notebooks showed that they were closely observing the world around them; for example, entries described the sound of the wind and a conversation between a father and an uncle.

Mrs. Nakamura and her colleagues had been following the constructivist or balanced literacy curriculum developed at KEEP (Au, Scheu, Kawakami, & Herman, 1990). This curriculum required teachers to grapple with a new philosophy of literacy and learning as well as new forms of instruction, classroom organization, and assessment. The 160 teachers who worked with the KEEP curriculum taught at 10 public schools in low-income communities on three of the Hawaiian Islands. The teachers varied considerably in years of classroom experience, ranging from zero to more than 20. All had volunteered to work with the KEEP curriculum because of their interest in improving their students' achievement. Teachers were encouraged to adopt new ideas and practices through extensive opportunities for staff development. KEEP consultants stationed in the schools conducted workshops, facilitated discussions among small groups of teachers, provided individual consultation, and assisted teachers with portfolio assessment.

The overarching goal of the curriculum was ownership of literacy. *Ownership* was defined as students' valuing of literacy, including holding positive attitudes toward literacy and having the habit of using literacy in everyday life. Students display positive attitudes by willingly engaging in reading and writing, showing confidence and pride in their own literacy, and taking an interest in the literacy of others (for example, by writing on the comment page of another student's published book). Students show that they have the habit of literacy when they read books at home, write in journals or diaries, maintain books of addresses and phone numbers, make lists, create greeting cards, and correspond with friends and relatives. Some of these activities (such as journal writing) may have been introduced by teachers, but students who have the habit of literacy engage in these activities outside of school when they are not required to. These actions show that students routinely engage in literacy even when not being supervised by teachers.

In the KEEP literacy curriculum a reciprocal relationship was assumed between ownership of literacy and proficiency in reading and writing. Students who have ownership of literacy are motivated to learn to read and write well, because literacy plays a central and meaningful role in their lives. Also, as students become more proficient at reading and writing, these activities can be carried out with greater ease and success, so they become more motivating.

Throughout the year Mrs. Nakamura conducted a writers' workshop nearly every day, giving students time to write on self-selected topics. During the second semester, she began the workshop by having students discuss experiences they might want to write about in their notebooks. Ten minutes of sustained silent writing followed, then the students gathered on the carpet, and five or six shared their notebook entries. Mrs. Nakamura taught them to comment on what was effective about the writer's approach. After the students read their entries, Mrs. Nakamura conducted a minilesson. Most often, as seen in the minilesson based on Nathan's writing, she taught about the author's craft and the qualities of effective writing, although she also covered skills such as spelling, punctuation, and capitalization. After the minilesson, students worked on their projects. Mrs. Nakamura taught them to go back through their notebooks and mark entries that might serve as the basis for projects, following the approach described by Calkins (1991).

The writers' workshop in Mrs. Nakamura's classroom serves as an example of the kind of highly engaging experiences that promote literacy learning in school. Although such experiences are beneficial to all students, they play a crucial role in the school literacy learning of students such as Nathan, who are of diverse backgrounds, as defined in Chapter 2. As discussed earlier, a gap between the literacy achievement of students of diverse backgrounds and students of mainstream backgrounds has long been documented, and educators face the challenge of considering how this gap can be bridged. In this chapter I take a close look at the relationship between motivation and the literacy achievement gap.

ANTHROPOLOGICAL PERSPECTIVES

The ideas of two educational anthropologists, John Ogbu and Frederick Erickson, serve as useful starting points for thinking about issues of motivation and their relation to the literacy achievement gap. Ogbu's (1990, 1993) theory is based on comparative research that addresses the question of why some students of diverse backgrounds succeed in school and others do not. Of relevance here are Ogbu's ideas about the achievement of students that he terms "castelike" or "involuntary minorities." He asserts that involuntary minorities became part of American society against their will through processes of enslavement, conquest, or colonization. Examples of such groups are African Americans and Native Hawaiians. Ogbu questions why involuntary minorities may not be motivated to overcome barriers to school success in the same way as immigrant or voluntary minorities. It should be noted that Ogbu's research addresses broad patterns of achievement and that other researchers (e.g., Achor & Morales, 1990; Hayes, 1992) have identified exceptions to these patterns and argued in favor of other theoretical perspectives.

In research conducted in Stockton, California, Ogbu (1981) identified economic incentive as one source of this lack of motivation. He documented the existence of a job ceiling that consigned African Americans to low-paying, low-status jobs regardless of the level of education they had achieved. In other words, education did not seem to yield the same benefits to African Americans as it did to European Americans in this study. African American parents told interviewers that they thought education to be important to their children's success in life. However, according to Ogbu, parents actually did not believe their children had the same chance to succeed as European Americans. For this reason, they did not strongly support their children's efforts to perform well academically.

Another barrier noted by Ogbu is the distrust of the public schools among involuntary minorities such as African Americans. This distrust, grounded in historical conditions of discrimination, leads some parents to conclude that public schools, particularly in the inner city, cannot provide their children with a proper education. These parents believe that public schools represent the same mainstream interests that have discriminated against involuntary minorities in the past.

Over time, discrimination and distrust contribute to the development of cultural practices that oppose ways of thinking common in the American mainstream, a phenomenon Ogbu (1993) terms "cultural inversion." Failing to do well in school appears to be an example of cultural inversion among involuntary minority students. To be successful in school, some African American high school students find that they must adopt a European American perspective or "act White" (Fordham, 1991). Many students appear unwilling to drop the markers of cultural identity that they associate with being African American as the price for school success. They generally believe that remaining part of the peer group and retaining ties with the community require that they not "act White" and, therefore, not be successful in school.

The research of Ogbu and his colleagues suggests that some involuntary minority students and their families have come to perceive schooling as a process of giving up their cultural identity without the guarantee of the social and economic rewards available to members of the mainstream. In this context educators must work to gain students' trust so that students become willing to acquire the strategies and attitudes necessary for academic success.

While Ogbu's research addresses factors in the larger society, Erickson's (1993; Erickson & Mohatt, 1982) research looks at face-to-face interactions in classrooms. Erickson argues that the school success or failure of students of diverse backgrounds is not simply predetermined by broad societal factors but results from the day-to-day interactions of students and teachers in the classroom. He suggests that students will be motivated to learn in school if teachers use communication patterns responsive to or compatible with the norms, beliefs, and values of students' home cultures. The use of such communication patterns is one form of culturally responsive instruction,as discussed at length in Chapter 3. Students' motivation increases because they understand the rules for participation and are able to engage comfortably and successfully in classroom activities.

An example of cultural responsiveness in communication patterns is seen in research on the use of talk-story-like participation structures in reading lessons with young Hawaiian children, introduced in Chapter 1. Au and Mason (1981, 1983) compared the lessons given by two teachers similar in professional background and years of teaching experience, with the notable difference that one (Teacher HC) had previously taught Hawaiian children while the other (Teacher LC) had not. Each teacher taught two lessons on reading comprehension to the same group of six Hawaiian second graders. Teacher HC, as expected, conducted her lessons following interactional rules similar to those in talk story, a Hawaiian community speech event (Watson, 1975). She did not tightly control turn taking but allowed the children to determine who would answer to her questions. Although she occasionally called on a particular child to speak, she did not prevent others from adding to that child's answer. The tone of the lessons was conversational, and there was considerable overlapping speech. The high level of collaboration shown in the lessons, which centered on group rather than individual performance, seemed consistent with the importance placed on cooperation versus competition in the students' home culture.

In contrast, Teacher LC conducted her lessons according to interactional rules typical in mainstream classrooms. She taught following the IRE (initiation-response-evaluation) pattern (Cazden, 1988; Mehan, 1979) in which the teacher initiates the topic, often through a question, and calls on a single student to respond. The chosen student is understood to have exclusive speaking rights, and others are not supposed to answer. The teacher evaluates the students' response, indicating whether it is correct.

Although this pattern for organizing interaction runs smoothly in mainstream classrooms, it did not work well in Teacher LC's lessons with Hawaiian children. When Teacher LC called upon a student to respond, others would add their ideas. It took Teacher LC a great deal of time to stop the other students from answering. As a result, she spent considerable time managing the lesson and little time discussing the story. The lessons moved forward fitfully, as the teacher attempted to enforce her rules for turn taking, which the students persisted in ignoring. The rules for the IRE pattern are rooted in norms of individual achievement and competition, values more important in mainstream culture than in the Hawaiian children's home culture.

The results showed that the students were much more attentive and involved in the lessons with the culturally responsive, talk-story-like participation structures than in the lessons with the IRE structure. Further, they discussed many more text ideas and made more logical inferences during the talk-story-like reading lessons. Reading lessons in which interaction was structured in a culturally responsive manner seemed to confer motivational and academic benefits on Hawaiian children that conventional reading lessons did not.

Erickson (1993) discusses why an adaptation as simple as changing the structure of turn taking in a lesson might promote the motivation and academic learning of students of diverse backgrounds. From an anthropological perspective, such adaptations may reduce the cultural shock in the classroom, as students find that familiar ways of speaking are accepted in an otherwise unfamiliar setting. In a symbolic sense, students may perceive the teacher's acceptance of their norms for interaction as affirming their own worth and the worth of their community.

Students are always doing some kind of learning, whether they are in school or in the community. According to Erickson, when educators say that students are "not learning," they mean that students are not learning the academic content being presented by teachers. Erickson views students' not learning—or more accurately, refusal to learn—as a form of political resistance. Students resist because they do not trust their teachers to exercise authority in a fair manner. Students must believe that assenting to the authority of teachers will prove beneficial rather than harmful to them, and they must feel that they can trust the teacher to respect their identities.

In situations where mutual trust is lacking, students become increasingly alienated from school, as Erickson (1993) suggests:

> It is no longer a matter of difference between teacher and student that derives from intergenerationally transmitted communicative traditions. It is also a matter of cultural intention as a medium of resistance in a situation of political conflict. As students grow older and experience repeated failure and repeated negative encounters with teachers, they develop oppositional cultural patterns as a symbol of their disaffiliation with what they experience (not necessarily within full reflective awareness) as an illegitimate and oppressive system. The more alienated the students become, the less they persist in doing schoolwork. Thus they fall farther and farther behind in academic achievement. The student becomes either actively resistant—seen as salient and incorrigible—or passively resistant—fading into the woodwork as an anonymous well-behaved, low-achieving student. (p. 41)

Erickson relates Ogbu's notion of cultural inversion to students' resistance to school and highlights the reflexive nature of school failure. Teachers' constant repetition of detrimental classroom situations triggers resistance, and students refuse to engage in the academic work that leads to school success. Teacher and students thus collaborate to perpetuate a cycle of failure (McDermott & Gospodinoff, 1981).

In short, Erickson (1993) argues that school failure is not a faceless process carried forward by the grand sweep of social and economic forces. Rather, the alienation of students of diverse backgrounds comes about through daily interactions between teachers and students in classrooms which tend first to lower students' motivation to do well in school and then to foster resistance. Teachers may well carry out hegemonic practices without conscious awareness or intent, but if they are inadvertently engaging in practices that put students of diverse backgrounds at a disadvantage, they can also decide to engage in alternative practices that build toward school success.

FINDINGS FROM RESEARCH
WITH NATIVE HAWAIIAN STUDENTS

Native Hawaiians fit Ogbu's characterization of involuntary minorities. Following the overthrow of the monarchy in 1893, Hawai'i ceased to be an independent kingdom and was annexed to the United States. As a result, the curriculum and instruction experienced by Hawaiian children during the 20th century have tended to reflect the beliefs and practices of the American mainstream. The consequences have not been positive. As a group, Hawaiian students in public schools in the state of Hawai'i score in the bottom quartile on standardized tests of reading achievement (Kamehameha Schools, 1993). Not surprisingly, they often exhibit negative attitudes toward reading and writing in the classroom.

Yet some teachers, such as Mrs. Nakamura, who worked with the KEEP literacy curriculum, have been able to create classrooms in which Hawaiian students show positive attitudes and considerable proficiency in literacy. Detailed reports of the five years of research with the curriculum are available elsewhere (Au & Asam, 1996; Au & Carroll, 1997; Au & Scheu, 1996; Carroll, Wilson, & Au, 1996). The remainder of this chapter will highlight findings from this research regarding issues of motivation and their relation to the literacy achievement gap.

Ownership as the Overarching Goal

As seen in Figure 5.1, the KEEP literacy curriculum incorporated six aspects of literacy, with ownership as the overarching goal (Au, Scheu, Kawakami, & Herman, 1990). Ownership was defined in the manner discussed earlier in this chapter.

Figure 5.1. Six Aspects of Literacy

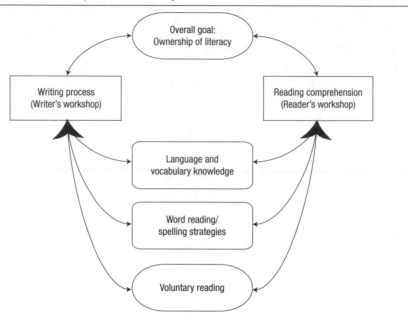

The second aspect of literacy was the writing process. In keeping with the process approach to writing, described by Graves (1983), Atwell (1987), Calkins (1994), and others, writing was viewed as a dynamic, recursive process involving planning, drafting, revising, editing, and publishing. Teachers conducted writers' workshops similar to that described in Mrs. Nakamura's classroom. Students wrote on self-selected topics, engaged in conferences with the teacher and with peers, and often published three or more books during the academic year.

Reading comprehension, the third aspect of literacy, was seen as a dynamic interaction among the reader, the text, and the social context in which reading took place (Wixson, Peters, Weber, & Roeber, 1987). The view of reading comprehension in the KEEP literacy curriculum followed reader response theory, particularly the ideas of Rosenblatt (1978, 1991). Teachers organized instruction around readers' workshops and encouraged students to develop personal responses to literature and to read from both aesthetic and efferent stances. Students wrote in response to literature and engaged in literature discussions, some teacher-led and others peer-guided.

The fourth aspect of literacy, language and vocabulary knowledge, referred to the ability to understand and use appropriate terms and structures in both spoken and printed English. Vocabulary was viewed in terms of knowledge of various topics (Mezynski, 1983), and teachers taught students the meanings of sets of words drawn from literature. For a work of fiction, there might be a set of words describing the characters' feelings, and for a work of nonfiction, a set of words associated with a topic such as volcanoes.

The treatment of word reading and spelling strategies, the fifth aspect of literacy, was based on Clay's (1985) idea that effective word identification requires using information from three cue systems: meaning (passage and sentence context), structural, and visual. Teachers taught word identification lessons based on opportunities afforded by the literature students were reading. For example, a particular text might present students with several compound words, words beginning with blends, or verbs ending with *-ing*. Spelling was taught primarily as part of editing during the writing process.

Voluntary reading, the sixth aspect of literacy, emphasized students' willingness to read independently from self-selected materials. Teachers promoted voluntary reading through read alouds, book talks, and daily periods of sustained silent reading. Classrooms contained well-stocked libraries with books of varying difficulty levels. Many teachers also encouraged students to read books of their own choosing at home.

In brief, the KEEP literacy curriculum encompassed both cognitive and affective dimensions of literacy and traditional skill areas as well as processes of meaning making and interpretation. Proficiency in literacy was certainly desired, but ownership was considered the primary goal. Each of the other aspects of literacy was thought to be related to ownership in the manner indicated by the arrows shown in Figure 5.1. The arrows pointing upward reflected the notion that ownership could be bolstered by the writing process and reading comprehension, which were reinforced by language and vocabulary knowledge, word identification and spelling strategies, and voluntary reading. The arrows pointing downward were intended to highlight the reciprocal nature of the relationship, the idea that ownership could increase student interest and commitment to engaging in the other five aspects of literacy.

The KEEP literacy curriculum proved highly effective in bringing issues of motivation to the forefront. Before this curriculum was adopted,

KEEP teachers and staff members had focused on proficiency in reading and writing as the endpoint. In implementing the KEEP literacy curriculum, they agreed that they would work toward helping students see literacy as a personally meaningful, significant part of their everyday lives, outside of school as well as within.

Using Motivating Classroom Activities

In classrooms where the majority of students are Hawaiian and from low-income families, resistance to schooling is common. D'Amato (1988) describes the phenomenon of "acting," a playful form of protest that can escalate to a tense, yearlong standoff between teacher and students. D'Amato points out that Hawaiian and other students of diverse backgrounds lack a structural rationale for complying with teacher's requests. Either they do not understand the structural relations between schooling and later life opportunities or they do not believe that doing well in school will affect their life opportunities. As Ogbu (1981) notes, a strong connection between doing well in school and obtaining a good job often has not been illustrated in their own family histories. Students who lack a structural rationale for cooperating with their teachers do not fear the consequences of poor academic achievement or disruptive behavior.

When a structural rationale is unavailable to students, D'Amato argues, teachers must provide a situational rationale. They must give students good reasons, within the classroom situation, for being cooperative and gaining proficiency in academic content and strategies. D'Amato endorses culturally responsive instruction as a means teachers can use to give students a situational rationale. Like Ogbu and Erickson, he recognizes the importance students attach to their cultural identities and peer group relationships.

In his research, D'Amato witnessed extraordinary efforts by Hawaiian students to maintain relationships of equality within the peer group. Students continually strived to show that they were just as good as everyone else, not to show that they were better. D'Amato notes that teacher use of the IRE structure forces students to perform and be judged as individuals, putting them in a situation where they must show that they are better than their peers. The use of talk-story-like participation structures is more effective with Hawaiian students, because it allows them to cooperate in producing answers and to maintain equality in peer relationships.

By using culturally responsive forms of instruction, teachers signal to students that they are in tune with them. Trust begins to develop as students realize that teachers are making it possible for them to succeed in school without having to violate cultural or peer group norms.

In addition to using culturally responsive forms of instruction, teachers can give students another kind of situational rationale: authentic, personally meaningful classroom experiences with literacy. In this regard, the process approach to writing has proved particularly effective in classrooms with Hawaiian students. An example of a writers' workshop following the process approach to writing is shown in the earlier description of Mrs. Nakamura's classroom. During whole-class and small-group discussions, Mrs. Nakamura often used talk-story-like participation structures. Students wrote on self-selected topics, first in their notebooks and then in the drafts of pieces they intended to publish. Mrs. Nakamura had students read aloud their drafts and published pieces in "The Author's Chair" (Graves & Hansen, 1983), so that students could be recognized as authors by the whole class. A bulletin board showed a photo of each student with the titles of his or her published books.

KEEP teachers such as Mrs. Nakamura took to heart Graves' (1990) notion that teachers must explore and share their own literacy with their students. Mrs. Nakamura shared her own writing with students, ranging from childhood memories of trying to trap mynah birds to recent events such as getting a flat tire on the freeway. She conducted minilessons in which she shared her drafts and revisions with students, pointing out how she crossed out words or whole sections and sometimes even had to start over again. She asked students for suggestions about how she might improve her drafts. Through these actions, Mrs. Nakamura showed that she too was a writer and put herself in the same vulnerable situation as her students. Trust developed as she and the students learned more about one another through sharing their writing, and students' motivation to write increased.

Assessing Growth in Ownership of Literacy

The KEEP literacy curriculum included portfolio assessment of the six aspects of literacy. Although affective aspects of literacy such as ownership and voluntary reading are not typically assessed, KEEP staff members decided to do so. They reasoned that ownership might not receive much attention unless it was assessed, because what gets assessed is often what gets taught.

KEEP staff members created grade-level benchmarks for ownership of literacy, based on classroom observations and teacher judgment about the kinds of habits and attitudes that should be expected at each grade level. The ownership benchmarks for Grades K–6 are shown in Figure 5.2. The benchmarks represent the habits and attitudes desired of the average student at the end of each grade level. Benchmarks were also created for the other five aspects of literacy (Asam et al., 1993).

KEEP staff members and teachers devised various means of assessing students' accomplishment of the ownership benchmarks. They used checklists or anecdotal records and kept artifacts (for example, notes children had written at home). They interviewed younger children or had older ones complete questionnaires. As they gathered evidence to document progress in meeting the benchmarks, KEEP teachers and staff members gained a keen awareness of the habits and attitudes associated with ownership of literacy. They then passed this awareness on to students. For example, teachers encouraged students to recommend books to others and to read books aloud to their younger siblings.

Leading Students to High Degrees of Ownership

By the second year of implementation of the KEEP literacy curriculum, improvements in the children's ownership of literacy were apparent to teachers and observers. Teachers had succeeded in engaging students in the full processes of reading and writing. Students discussed novels with

Figure 5.2. Benchmarks for Ownership of Literacy

			Grade Level				
Ownership of Writing	K	1	2	3	4	5	6
Enjoys writing	X	X	X	X	X	X	X
Shows confidence and pride in own writing	X	X	X	X	X	X	X
Shares own writing with others	X	X	X	X	X	X	X
Shows interest in others' writing	X	X	X	X	X	X	X
Writes in class for own purposes		X	X	X	X	X	X
Writes outside of class for own purposes			X	X	X	X	X
Makes connections between reading and writing				X	X	X	X
Sets goals and evaluates own achievement of writing					X	X	X
Gains insights through writing						X	X

the teacher and their peers, wrote in response to literature, and had time to read books they had chosen. They wrote on self-selected topics and shared their writing with others. They were actively engaged in meaningful literacy activities within classroom communities of learners.

During the second and third years of implementation of the KEEP literacy curriculum, results were collected for all students in kindergarten through Grade 3 at the nine schools, a total of about 2,000. About two thirds of the students were of Native Hawaiian ancestry, and the majority of them were from low-income families. During the school year, portfolios were assembled for each student, containing evidence of progress in meeting the grade-level benchmarks in each of the six aspects of literacy. For example, observational checklists, interviews, and anecdotal records were collected as evidence of ownership, and written summaries and reading logs were collected as evidence of reading comprehension.

By referring to the evidence in students' portfolios and the grade-level benchmarks, KEEP teachers and staff members could rate students as below, at, or above grade level in the aspects of literacy. Students received a rating of *below grade level* in a particular aspect of literacy if their portfolios did not show evidence that they had met all the benchmarks for their grade level. They received a rating of *at grade level* if there was evidence that they had met all the benchmarks. To be rated *above grade level*, a student had to have portfolio evidence meeting all the benchmarks for the next higher grade. Baseline portfolio data had not been collected prior to implementation of the KEEP literacy curriculum, so it was not possible to make comparisons to students' previous levels of achievement. However, the results for each classroom were audited for the adequacy of evidence in students' portfolios and for the accuracy of ratings.

Observers' impressions of the classrooms were confirmed in the assessment results for ownership of literacy, which indicated that about two thirds of the students in kindergarten through Grade 3 had met the benchmarks at their grade level. The KEEP literacy curriculum appeared to be leading to high levels of engagement in literacy among students of diverse backgrounds. As discussed below, however, this finding tells only part of the story.

Ownership and Proficiency

The 2 years of data previously discussed indicated that KEEP students had not reached adequate levels of proficiency in reading and writing, as measured by grade-level benchmarks. Across all grade levels, approximately two thirds of the students were rated below grade level in the writing process and in reading comprehension. Students also remained below grade level in vocabulary and language development; assessment in this area was closely tied to assessment of reading comprehension. These aspects of literacy required complex forms of higher-level thinking that did not develop simply as a consequence of students' high engagement with literacy. Interestingly, proficiency in word identification did reach acceptable levels, perhaps due to high levels of voluntary reading (for complete results, refer to Au & Asam, 1996; Au & Carroll, 1997).

These findings indicated that students appeared to require extensive instruction in the complex kinds of thinking involved in the writing process and reading comprehension. While ownership and proficiency were undoubtedly related, the two were not perfectly correlated. Proficiency in literacy did not follow naturally as a consequence of high degrees of ownership.

Aiming Toward High Standards

In the fourth and fifth years of work with the literacy curriculum, KEEP staff members focused on achieving implementation of the curriculum in just a few demonstration classrooms, to determine whether better achievement results could be attained. Thirteen demonstration teachers participated in the fourth year and 30 in the fifth year. (Mrs. Nakamura became a demonstration teacher in the fifth year, when the observations reported here were made.) The demonstration teachers were asked to concentrate either on implementation of the writers' workshop or the readers' workshop, and the majority chose the writers' workshop. The following discussion will address the work of the writing-oriented teachers (11 in the fourth year and 26 in the fifth year).

The demonstration teachers provided instruction in the writing process within the context of having students write on self-selected topics. For the most part, the teachers knew how to conduct minilessons and conferences. However, they had difficulty making their own writing part of instruction. The teachers who, like Mrs. Nakamura, had the courage to use samples of their own writing in minilessons, discovered that they were better able to motivate students to learn and apply the targeted concepts, strategies, and skills. By revealing their own struggles as writers, teachers made the minilessons meaningful to students (Au & Scheu, 1996).

The teachers also worked on portfolio assessment. As they monitored students' progress toward the benchmarks, teachers gained information that led to adjustments in instruction. For example, a second-grade teacher noticed that the majority of her students were not meeting the benchmarks for editing. She realized that she had been taking much of the responsibility for editing upon herself. To remedy the situation, she began conducting a series of minilessons on editing skills. At the same time, she required students to attempt to edit their own pieces and to work with a peer editor before she met with them for an editing conference.

The teachers engaged older students (from the second grade and higher) in the process of gathering evidence to show that they were meeting the benchmarks. A fifth-grade teacher identified the benchmarks she would focus on for the first quarter, second quarter, and so on. For example, benchmarks for planning and drafting seemed achievable during the first quarter, while those for publishing were put off until later in the year. Near the end of the first quarter, the teacher showed a group of six students how to label evidence in their portfolios to show that they had met the first-quarter benchmarks. These students worked with small groups of classmates to teach them the same process. In 2 days, all students in the class had assessed their own progress toward meeting the first-quarter benchmarks. They knew which benchmarks they had achieved and which still required work. The teacher had the students repeat the process of self-evaluation toward the end of the second, third, and fourth quarters. Not surprisingly, most of her students succeeded in meeting all the fifth-grade benchmarks for ownership of writing and the writing process by the end of the year.

During the fourth and fifth years, the demonstration teachers achieved outstanding results. In both years over 80% of their students received ratings of at or above grade level in ownership of writing. More important, during both years about 66% of the students were rated at or above grade level in the writing process. These results were the opposite of those obtained during the first 3 years of implementation, when about 67% of the students had been rated below grade level in the writing process (for details of the results, refer to Au & Asam, 1996; Au & Carroll, 1997.)

Through a combination of intensive instruction and close monitoring of student progress toward the benchmarks, the demonstration teachers showed that the KEEP literacy curriculum could be effective in improving students' literacy achievement in terms of the quality of students' writing and their ownership of literacy.

CONCLUSION

Students of diverse backgrounds may lack the motivation to do well in school because, in their family histories, success in school has not led to better life opportunities. Further, students may decide not to be successful in school if they have to give up their cultural identities. To motivate students of diverse backgrounds, teachers must explore alternatives that allow students to be successful in school while maintaining their cultural identities. Two interrelated approaches appear promising: culturally responsive instruction (Key to Success #3) and instruction centered on authentic literacy activities.

Making ownership of literacy the overarching goal of the curriculum can be a first step toward improving the literacy achievement of students of diverse backgrounds. However, high levels of motivation will not automatically lead to increased achievement. Efforts to increase students' ownership of literacy must be combined with high standards (for example, in the form of grade-level benchmarks) and intense instruction in the higher-level thinking processes required in the writing process and in reading comprehension, in keeping with Key to Success #2. Only then can the literacy achievement gap be bridged.

FOLLOW-UP ACTIVITY

Reflect on the approaches to literacy learning in place at your school or a school you know well. These approaches might range from instructional frameworks, such as the writers' and readers' workshops, to packaged programs, such as basal readers. What were the reasons for selecting these particular approaches? In your judgment, what are the strengths and weaknesses of these approaches? What have been the effects on students' literacy learning? If you and your colleagues were going to provide the powerful instruction needed to bring students to high levels of literacy, what would you keep the same? What would you do differently?

Chapter 6

Balanced Literacy Instruction: Implications for Students of Diverse Backgrounds

The place of phonics and basic skills must necessarily be addressed in detail in discussions of solutions to the literacy achievement gap. As indicated by Key to Success #1, the gap is complexly determined, and skill instruction is one of the areas that requires careful thought and attention. In this chapter I tackle this often contentious topic by beginning with a discussion of dimensions to be balanced within balanced literacy instruction. I highlight the dimension of skill contextualization as particularly significant in the effective early literacy instruction of children of diverse backgrounds. Focusing on the primary grades, this chapter is structured around six research-based generalizations about effective literacy instruction. These include the idea that students of diverse backgrounds benefit from the opportunity to use invented spelling, when they can infer for themselves how letters go together to form words in English.

Another idea is that teachers should follow a continuum of instructional strategies, shifting strategies to match students' changing needs as literacy learners. The overarching concept is that students require instruction that allows them to engage in authentic literacy activities. I propose that, once motivated to read and write for purposes they find meaningful, students of diverse backgrounds will be able to acquire all the literacy skills and strategies they need for success in school and beyond.

One of the ideas I hope you will take from this chapter is that higher-level thinking, in the form of reasoning about text, should be part of word identification, as indicated by Key to Success #2. All students, including students of diverse backgrounds, need the opportunity to learn how to use reasoning when dealing with decodable words.

Few topics, if any, in the field of language arts have been as contentious as beginning reading. In the 1960s, Chall (1967) used the phrase *great
debate* to characterize the disagreements between proponents of code-
emphasis versus meaning-emphasis approaches. In the 1990s, the popular press used the phrase *reading wars* to describe the arguments between
proponents of phonics versus whole language (Collins, 1997). Continuing
media coverage of the so-called reading wars served to obscure the fact
that the majority of classroom teachers and literacy researchers did not fall
into either of the extreme camps. For example, results of a large-scale survey indicated that 89% of elementary teachers held a balanced or eclectic
philosophy, as reflected in the statement, "I believe in a balanced approach
to reading instruction which combines skills development with literature
and language-rich activities" (Baumann, Hoffman, Moon, & Duffy-Hester,
1998, p. 642). Prominent researchers agreed that emphasizing only phonics instruction would make learning to read difficult and that children
should read and discuss a wide variety of texts (Flippo, 1998). By the mid-
1990s this seldom heard majority had begun to articulate a position known
as *balanced literacy instruction.*

My purpose in this chapter is to present a perspective on balanced literacy instruction that I hope will be especially helpful to those who work,
as I do, with students of diverse cultural and linguistic backgrounds. I begin
by looking at different dimensions of balance in literacy instruction. Then
I examine the intersection of three topics that have figured prominently in
recent debates about literacy instruction: constructivist approaches, phonics and skills, and the literacy learning of students of diverse backgrounds.

BALANCED LITERACY INSTRUCTION

Pearson and Raphael (1999) provided a comprehensive discussion of *balance*, unpacking the term by referring to continua in the context and content of literacy instruction. Within the context of literacy instruction, the
first continuum is authenticity, with the need to achieve a balance between
"doin' school" and "doin' life." The second continuum is classroom discourse, with the need to achieve a balance between the rights of teachers
and of children to determine the topics discussed and the patterns of classroom talk. The third continuum is the teacher's role, which can range from
minimal (the teacher joins the students in participating in a literacy activ-

ity such as sustained silent reading) to maximum (the teacher uses explicit instruction). The final context continuum is curricular control, with the need to achieve a balance between local control by educators in the classroom and distant control at the state or national level.

Pearson and Raphael (1999) highlighted three continua in the area of content. Skill contextualization refers to maintaining a balance between a predetermined curriculum of skill instruction and the teaching of skills as teachable moments are provided by texts and tasks. Text genres refers to maintaining a balance between the reading of narrative as opposed to informational texts, as well as a balance between the reading of texts written to support the practice of beginning reading skills versus authentic texts, such as children's literature. The final continuum, response to literature, refers to maintaining a balance between conventional or canonical interpretations and students' personal interpretations. In short, these authors suggested that the concept of balanced literacy instruction has at least seven dimensions.

As the analysis by Pearson and Raphael (1999) suggested, balanced literacy instruction is a complex concept. Furthermore, other dimensions can easily be added. For example, Strickland (1994) addressed the dimensions of ability versus heterogeneous grouping and standardized versus ongoing classroom assessment. Spiegel (1998) emphasized the role of the teacher as a reflective practitioner and decision maker in finding the best way to help each child become a better reader and writer. Freppon and Dahl (1998) pointed out that although there is wide agreement on the benefits of phonics instruction, there is no consensus about how this instruction should take place. They found that "several balanced literacy researchers repeatedly emphasize the importance of phonics teaching and learning within integrated language-based instruction; however, others argued for separating phonics teaching and learning" (p. 247).

I call here for consideration of still another dimension of balance, and that is between the demands of the mainstream language arts curriculum and the needs in learning to read and write of children of diverse cultural and linguistic backgrounds. This dimension intersects all of the continua proposed by Pearson and Raphael (1999) and brings to the fore issues of authenticity, classroom discourse, curricular control, and response to literature. However, the predominant continuum of balance in my discussion will be skill contextualization. In keeping with the issue raised by Freppon and Dahl (1998) about how phonics instruction should take place, I argue that such instruction is more likely to be effective for many children of diverse backgrounds when it is integrated into language-based instruction.

RESEARCH WITH HAWAIIAN CHILDREN

My perspective on balanced literacy instruction has been shaped by the many years that I spent working at the Kamehameha Elementary Education Program (KEEP) in Hawai'i. As mentioned in Chapter 1, the purpose of KEEP was to improve the literacy achievement of students of Hawaiian ancestry enrolled in public schools. I do not support a narrow focus on "back-to-basics" instruction because my research with Hawaiian students has shown me that phonics is just one part of children's literacy learning during the early years of elementary school. It is an essential part but, as I will explain, neither the starting point nor the most important element.

In this chapter I draw on three sources of information. The first is research at KEEP on a constructivist literacy curriculum. As discussed in Chapter 1, KEEP was established in 1971 and became the nation's longest running research and development project dedicated to improving the educational opportunities of underprivileged students of a particular ethnic group. From 1989 to 1995, the year KEEP closed, my colleagues and I conducted research on the constructivist literacy curriculum, centered on writers' and readers' workshops, described in Chapter 5. The second source of information is the larger body of research conducted by others, and the third is the experience of the teachers with whom I have worked.

DEFINITION OF TERMS

Constructivist approaches to literacy research refers to approaches based on the idea that students create their own understandings of literacy in the context of the various aspects of their lives (Spivey, 1997). The assumption in these approaches is that learning takes place through social interaction with peers as well as the teacher. The teacher initiates instruction by getting students interested and involved in the full processes of reading and writing, and skills are taught as part of students' engagement with meaningful literacy activities. Constructivist approaches to literacy instruction include the process approach to writing (Calkins, 1994; Graves, 1983, 1994), literature-based instruction (Raphael &

Au, 1998; Roser & Martinez, 1995), whole language (Goodman, 1986; Weaver, 1990), and balanced literacy instruction (Au, Carroll, & Scheu, 1997; Strickland, 1994–95). These approaches and philosophies are consistent with a constructivist or interpretivist paradigm (Guba & Lincoln, 1994; Spivey, 1997) and the sociocultural or sociohistorial perspective, as exemplified in the work of Vygotsky (1978) and discussed in Chapter 2. These perspectives have been extended to literacy research and education by Applebee (1991), Brock and Gavelek (1998), Cole and Griffin (1983), Moll (1990), Raphael and Hiebert (1996), and others.

Phonics refers to the teaching of letter-sound correspondences. The term is also commonly used to refer to the letter-sound correspondences themselves, as in the phrase "phonics instruction" or in the statement "Children need to know phonics." Phonics is valuable because English is an alphabetic language, and knowledge of letter-sound correspondences helps students to decode words. However, phonics is not the only type of word identification instruction that students should receive. Students also need to learn to recognize words that are not decodable (a category that includes many of the most frequently occurring words), to analyze multisyllabic words, and to make use of base words and affixes.

Constructivist approaches provide us with many powerful ways to improve the literacy instruction of students of diverse backgrounds. In Chapter 5 I explained my reasons for recommending a constructivist process approach to writing, in the form of the writers' workshop, as the starting point for literacy instruction in classrooms with students of diverse backgrounds. In this chapter I focus primarily on a constructivist approach to the teaching of reading and literature-based instruction. This information is organized according to six understandings I have gained about these issues, drawing from my own research as well as the research of others.

FINDINGS FROM RESEARCH

Ownership of Literacy as the Overarching Goal

The first understanding has to do with the breadth of the elementary language arts curriculum and the shift from reading, narrowly defined, to literacy, broadly defined. As indicated in Chapter 5, the researchers at KEEP worked with a curriculum with six aspects of literacy: ownership, the writing process, reading comprehension, vocabulary development, word reading and spelling strategies, and voluntary reading (Au, Scheu, Kawakami, & Herman, 1990). This curriculum recognized the connections between reading and writing and the importance of affective dimensions of literacy as well as cognitive ones.

Perhaps the most important discovery was that ownership of literacy needed to be the overarching goal of the curriculum. As discussed in Chapters 2 and 5, ownership is seen when students not only have positive attitudes about literacy but make it a part of their everyday lives, at home as well as in school. Students demonstrate ownership by reading books of their own choosing, keeping journals, and sharing books with one another, even when these activities are not assigned by the teacher. They use reading and writing for purposes they have set for themselves. Winograd and Paris (1988) espoused a similar view when they wrote about students needing to have the will as well as the skill to use literacy. Dahl and Freppon (1995) suggested that acquiring a "disposition for learning" and thinking of oneself as a reader and writer may be a critical occurrence during inner-city children's beginning years in school. The importance of ownership is supported in research on the engagement perspective by Guthrie and Alvermann (1999) and their colleagues. The engagement perspective looks beyond the question of *how* people read to the question of *why* someone would want to read in the first place.

The view of the literacy curriculum reflected in the six aspects of literacy is largely process oriented, which I believe is typical of constructivist language arts curricula developed in the late 1980s and early 1990s. In subsequent years, views of the literacy curriculum shifted somewhat, as shown in Figure 6.1.

Two differences between Figure 5.1, which shows the six aspects of literacy, and Figure 6.1 should be noted. First, the label *literary aspects* in Figure 6.1 represents a recognition that the literacy curriculum must address content, not just process. Literary aspects include the themes developed through literature, or the ideas that hold the story together and that will be remembered long after details of the plot and setting have faded from memory (Lukens, 1990). The value of themes in literature-based instruction has been discussed in work by Peters and Wixson (1998) and Valencia and Lipson (1998). Literary elements also include point of view, plot, and characters. Of course, the purpose of addressing literary aspects is to enhance the reader's response to the literature, whether that response is personal, creative, or critical.

Figure 6.1. Current Literacy Curriculum

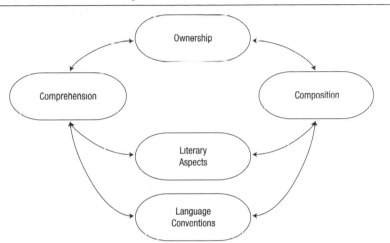

Source: From Au, K. H., & Raphael, T. E. (1998). Curriculum and Teaching in Literature-Based Programs. In T. E. Raphael & K. H. Au (Eds.), *Literature-based Instruction: Reshaping the Curriculum*, p. 128. Norwood, MA: Christopher-Gordon. Copyright ©1998. Reprinted with permission.

Second, the label *language conventions* in Figure 6.1 reflects the idea that literacy is a social process requiring interactional skills, not just text-based skills and strategies. This element encompasses the aspects of literacy represented in the KEEP framework by the labels *language and vocabulary knowledge* and *word reading and spelling strategies*. Besides addressing the traditional skill areas of vocabulary, word identification, grammar, punctuation, and other mechanics, this area deals with the conventions of interaction students must know in order to participate appropriately in literacy events. These conventions come into play in all literacy events but may be particularly complex in activities directed by the students themselves, such as literature discussion groups during the readers' workshop or peer conferences during the writers' workshop. Many of these language conventions may be more familiar to mainstream students than to students of diverse backgrounds.

In short, current research shows the breadth of the literacy curriculum. Many studies document the importance of all of these curriculum elements in students' development as readers and writers (Guthrie & Alvermann, 1999; Raphael & Au, 1998).

What is the place of phonics in this picture? Phonics is part of one of the five elements in the contemporary literacy curriculum. Phonics cannot be neglected, but there is no evidence to suggest that it can or should be the whole of reading, even at the kindergarten and first-grade levels. As discussed in Chapter 5, research conducted at KEEP indicated that students of diverse backgrounds may develop greater proficiency in word identification when instruction begins by promoting ownership and not just skills.

Improvement of Word Identification and Higher-Level Thinking

The second understanding concerns the importance of providing students at all grades with instruction in comprehension and composition, complex literacy processes requiring higher-level thinking. In our initial work with the constructivist curriculum at KEEP, we made an interesting discovery, as mentioned in Chapter 5. The results shown in Table 6.1 illustrate the pattern we observed for 2 consecutive years with nearly 2,000 students in six schools in Grades 1 through 3, as measured by a portfolio assessment system anchored in grade-level benchmarks (Au, 1994). We saw better achievement results in some aspects of literacy than in others. The results for these aspects of literacy are shown above the horizontal line in the center of the table, and they are ownership of literacy, voluntary reading, and word reading strategies. This is what seems to have happened. Teachers with KEEP focused on promoting students' ownership of literacy, and they encouraged students to read books at home as well as at school. They set aside time daily for sustained silent reading, and the vast majority of students developed the habit of daily reading. Because of this increase in independent reading, students' fluency and accuracy in word identification

Table 6.1. Initial Results: Grade 2

Aspect of Literacy	% Above	% At	% Below	Missing Data
Ownership	30	19	46	5
Voluntary reading	71	24	5	0
Word reading strategies	39	20	38	2
Writing process	0	33	55	11
Reading comprehension	5	31	59	5
Language and vocabulary	3	37	54	6

improved, as indicated in individually administered running records (Clay, 1985). We were particularly surprised to find 39% of the second graders performing above grade level, which in this case meant that they could accurately decode texts at the 3.2 (third grade, second semester) reading level. Achievement lagged in the other three aspects of literacy: the writing process, reading comprehension, and language and vocabulary knowledge.

These initial results show that gains in word identification were somewhat easier to obtain with constructivist curricula than gains in the more complex literacy processes—composition, comprehension, and the learning of concepts and vocabulary. With the KEEP students, and very likely with other students of diverse backgrounds, word identification was neither as difficult for teachers to teach nor as difficult for students to learn, as these more complex processes. In other words, our findings at KEEP contradict the impression that constructivist approaches are somehow detrimental to students' development of word identification ability. In our last 2 years of work with the constructivist curriculum at KEEP, we focused specifically on improving students' higher-level thinking about text, particularly in the writing process, as explained in Chapter 5. We learned that a constructivist curriculum could be effective in improving students' achievement in these areas but only when teachers fully implemented the curriculum (Au & Carroll, 1997). Narrowly focused basic skill instruction, unlike constructivist approaches, ignores the more complex literacy processes and therefore cannot lead to improvement in these processes.

Our research findings at KEEP will come as no surprise to those familiar with the extensive research base on comprehension instruction developed during the 1980s. We learned early on, most notably from a study conducted by Anderson, Mason, and Shirey (1984), that comprehension does not result naturally as a consequence of students being able to decode every word in a text. Researchers looked at the different kinds of challenges comprehension posed for students and how students might be taught to meet these challenges. They demonstrated that strategy instruction could improve students' comprehension, in terms of their ability to make inferences (Hansen & Pearson, 1983), identify the main idea (Baumann, 1984), or summarize a text (Taylor, 1982). Other studies pointed to the benefits of students being able to monitor their own comprehension—to know when they didn't know (Palincsar & Brown, 1984). This research on comprehension strategy instruction was ably summarized by Dole and colleagues (1991). Work by Beck, McKeown, Sandora, Kucan, and Worthy (1996), in which students are taught to "question the author," built on this foundation.

Concepts of comprehension have been enriched by continuing research on literature-based instruction (e.g., Sipe, 2008), which has its theoretical basis in reader response theory. Rosenblatt's (1978) work established the distinction between the aesthetic and efferent stances and argued persuasively for the predominance of the aesthetic stance in the reading of literature. Our views of what it means to comprehend have been broadened to encompass personal response, which includes the emotions called forth by the literature and the ability to see connections between literature and one's own life.

Timing of Phonics

The third understanding recognizes that although phonics has its place, it cannot be the first or only focus for beginning readers, particularly for young children of diverse backgrounds who have limited experienced with family storybook reading or other mainstream literacy events. The timing of phonics instruction for these children is critical. In fact, in kindergarten and first grade, an overemphasis on phonics instruction, to the exclusion of other literacy activities, may prevent these children from developing the concepts and background necessary for the later development of word identification ability.

This point is made clear in a discussion by Stahl (1997). Citing common findings in the work of a number of researchers (Biemiller, 1970; Chall, 1983; Frith, 1985; Lomax & McGee, 1987; McCormick & Mason, 1986), Stahl noted that children go through three broad stages in learning to identify words: awareness, accuracy, and automaticity

In the first stage, awareness, children are developing a conceptual understanding of the nature of written language and its relationship to spoken language. This understanding covers four areas: (1) Functions of print involves understanding, for example, that print can be used to tell stories; (2) conventions of print includes knowing that one reads from left to right and from the top of the page to the bottom; (3) forms of print encompasses the letters of the alphabet; and (4) awareness of phonemes entails the notion that spoken words can be broken into separate sounds or phonemes, an understanding central to the later learning of letter-sound correspondences. Stahl (1997) asserted that these four aspects of the relationship between written and spoken language serve as the foundation for children's later development as readers, and that children will experience difficulty in learning to read if they lack any of these aspects.

In the second stage, accuracy, children learn to decode words accurately. They are focused on print and working to identify words correctly. Sulzby (1985) described this as a time when children, who previously freely retold stories from familiar books, will refuse to do so, stating, "I don't know the words." Children read text aloud in a laborious, choppy, word-by-word fashion, a phenomenon usually termed *word calling.*

Stahl (1997) noted that the second stage is generally short-lived, leading quickly into the third stage, automaticity, in which children come to recognize words automatically. The transition from accuracy to automaticity usually occupies the time from the end of first grade to the end of third grade, although it may be prolonged for struggling readers. The rapid, automatic recognition of words is, of course, necessary to free up information processing capacity for comprehension of the text.

This overview of the development of word identification ability suggests that phonics instruction should be emphasized when children are in the accuracy phase, not when they are in the awareness phase and not when they are in the automaticity phase. Phonics plays a crucial but temporary role, and phonics instruction must be properly timed to achieve its optimal effect. Phonics cannot be seen as a blanket approach to beginning reading instruction, because knowledge of letter-sound correspondences is not the first or the only thing that children need to learn as they develop the ability to identify words.

In a conversation about research on emergent literacy in the *Reading Research Quarterly,* Purcell-Gates (McGee & Purcell-Gates, 1997) drew a conclusion that is not new but often forgotten in current debates: "Children learn to read and write successfully if their teachers accommodate their instruction *to* the children, and they struggle if they do not" (p. 312). This statement certainly applies to many young Hawaiian children, who are in the awareness stage when they first arrive in kindergarten. At KEEP we administered emergent literacy tasks (based on the work of Mason & Stewart, 1989) to children entering kindergarten. The typical child could name perhaps one to three letters of the alphabet, often letters that appeared in his or her name but could not use magnetic letters to represent the first or last sounds of any words. When shown the page of a simple book and asked where there was something to read, the typical child pointed to the illustration, not to the print. Clearly, the typical child was not yet attending to print. Many KEEP kindergartners had little or no experience with family storybook reading, and most had not attended preschool.

Unless there is good evidence that kindergarten children are already in or near the accuracy stage, it appears harmful to their overall literacy development to begin with an emphasis on the teaching of phonics in isolation. Some kindergarten teachers insist on drilling children on letter names and sounds in isolation, a form of teaching that is too abstract for many children. This type of teaching cannot replace instructional activities, such as shared reading or the writing of their own stories, which provide children with meaningful contexts for the learning of letter-sound correspondences. These activities allow children to develop understandings of the four aspects of written-spoken language relationships that form the foundation for later acquisition of letter-sound correspondences. Phonics instruction can certainly be introduced as part of shared reading and children's writing of their own stories, as I describe next, but phonics should not be taught apart from these meaningful literacy activities.

Writing and the Learning of Letter-Sound Correspondences

The fourth understanding concerns the contributions of writing, specifically invented spelling, to children's learning of phonics. In KEEP primary-grade classrooms, teachers conducted a writers' workshop four or five times a week. They introduced the writers' workshop as soon as possible, sometimes during the first day of school. This introduction required courage and faith on the part of teachers, especially in kindergarten classrooms. In September, most of these kindergarten students were drawing, and just a few were scribbling or using letterlike forms. In classrooms in rural schools, there was often a child who had not yet had the experience of holding a pencil or crayon and drawing with it.

During the writers' workshop, kindergarten teachers promoted children's understandings of print in many ways. They modeled writing during the morning message, asking children to help them spell the words, and had children make observations about the print in the message (Crowell, Kawakami, & Wong, 1986). They taught minilessons showing children how to say words slowly and isolate the sounds. They introduced children to the sounds and letters of the alphabet through lessons in which children associated letters with the names of their classmates or familiar objects. They created word walls and posted charts to which the children could refer, including lists of people (*mommy, brother, cousin*) and actions (*planting, surfing, rollerblading*). Gradually, teachers identified children who could use invented spelling to label objects in their drawings. During individual

or small-group writing conferences, they assisted these children with label-
ing and then taught them how to use initial consonants to draft short sentences. By the spring semester, most of the children in these kindergarten
classrooms were able to draft several sentences each day during the writers'
workshop, using at least initial consonants to represent words.

In my experience, the writers' workshop provides the best context in
which to teach children letter-sound correspondences—phonics—in a
manner that makes that knowledge useful and ensures its application. The
following summary of my observations in a kindergarten classroom provides a sense of how phonics fits within the larger context of meaningful
literate activity in the writers' workshop. In this classroom the teacher had
the children keep four questions in mind when they wrote their stories:

1. Who is in my story?
2. What is happening in my story?
3. Where is my story taking place?
4. What else happened?

She did not use the terms characters, events, and setting, but the children clearly understood these concepts. I observed a girl drafting the sentence, "I am popping firecrackers with my friends at home." The teacher
had taught the children to isolate the first sound in the word and write
that letter. Then they were to say the word slowly, listen for other sounds,
and add those letters. For example, the girl who wanted to write *popping*
isolated the initial p sound, said, "Puh-puh-puh" to herself, and wrote the
letter *p*. As this example shows, children in primary classrooms with writers' workshops create their own phonics exercises because of the stories
they want to write. The teacher in this classroom, along with many other
teachers, have told me words to this effect: "I have taught letter sounds in
isolation, and this way, through invented spelling, is much faster and more
effective."

My observations in classrooms with Hawaiian children are consistent
with a growing body of studies pointing to the benefits of invented spelling
in children's long-term development as readers and writers (Ehri, 1987;
Wilde, 1989). These studies suggest that children who have the opportunity to use invented spelling eventually become better spellers than children who are taught spelling by rote memorization and never have the
opportunity to infer for themselves how the English spelling system works.
In the case of both spelling and phonics, it is not just a matter of learning

skills but of applying these skills in the context of real reading and writing. Teachers commonly observe that students misspell words they wrote correctly on recent spelling tests. Similarly, it is likely that many children who learn phonics in isolation do not use these skills when they read (Shannon, 1989), and by fourth grade, students' reading problems are related to a lack of automaticity rather than to the absence of basic reading skills (Campbell & Ashworth, 1995).

Multipronged Approach to Phonics

There does not appear to be one best way to teach phonics and beginning reading (Allington, 1997). This assertion is supported by the fact that, for every method studied, some children learned to read well while others experienced considerable difficulty (International Reading Association, 1999). It can be concluded, then, that students of diverse backgrounds will benefit from a multipronged approach that shows them the usefulness of letter-sound correspondences during both reading and writing. Our research at KEEP supports this contention. Decoding by analogy is an approach to word identification, demonstrated to be effective (Gaskins, Gaskins, & Gaskins, 1991), that has undergone continual refinement (Gaskins, Ehri, Cress, O'Hara, & Donnelly, 1997). At KEEP we asked Pat Cunningham to provide workshops to our teachers on decoding by analogy, and KEEP teachers taught lessons incorporating word walls (Cunningham, 1991). The relative importance of onset-rime segmentation and phonemic segmentation in children's development of word reading and spelling ability continues to be explored in the experimental literature (e.g., Nation & Hulme, 1997). However, the KEEP students seemed to benefit both from learning decoding by analogy, which requires onset-rime segmentation, and from learning invented spelling, which led them to employ phonemic segmentation.

Although research suggests that there is no single best way to teach phonics, there do appear to be two principles that underlie effective phonics instruction for Hawaiian students and others of diverse backgrounds. The first principle is that phonics instruction should be explicit. In two controversial and widely cited articles in the *Harvard Educational Review,* Delpit (reprinted in Delpit, 1995) presented a convincing case for the explicit instruction of skills within constructivist approaches for students of diverse backgrounds. Delpit stated that, unlike their mainstream, middle-class peers, students of diverse backgrounds generally did not have the opportunity outside of the classroom to acquire the codes of the culture of power. These codes include such skills as phonics and standard English grammar. According to Delpit, teachers handicap students of diverse backgrounds when they fail to provide explicit instruction in these skills. As indicated above, teachers in KEEP classrooms provided students with explicit instruction in phonics through a wide variety of activities. Delpit described herself as a progressive educator, with a commitment to the process approach to writing, but she argued that explicit skill instruction should be a part of the process approach. Delpit (1988) added this caveat, with which I agree: "I am not an advocate of a simplistic 'basic skills' approach for children outside the culture of power. It would be (and has been) tragic to operate as if these children were incapable of critical and higher-order thinking and reasoning" (p. 286).

I hesitate to use the word *systematic* along with *explicit* because of the many misunderstandings of what *systematic* might mean when it comes to phonics instruction. There is no evidence for the effectiveness of phonics that is thought to be systematic because the teacher follows a set sequence of skill lessons. As Allington (1997) put it, "There simply is no 'scientifically' validated sequence of phonics instruction" (p. 15). This rigid concept should be replaced by one in which phonics is understood to be systematic because the teacher provides instruction based on ongoing assessment of the children's needs as readers and writers. Phonics should also be systematic in the sense that teachers devote considerable time and attention to it on a daily basis, when ongoing assessment indicates that such instruction will be beneficial to children.

The second principle is that this explicit phonics instruction should take place in meaningful contexts in which the reasons for learning letter-sound correspondences can readily be understood by children. In the writers' workshop, described earlier, children understand that they need knowledge of letter-sound correspondences to put their stories down on paper for communication to others. In shared reading and guided reading, children understand that knowledge of letter-sound correspondences enables them to read the words in books for themselves. Children are pursuing certain purposes through literacy and can see the value of knowledge of letter-sound correspondences in achieving these purposes.

McGee (in McGee & Purcell-Gates, 1997) presented a thoughtful discussion of these issues. She noted that "any understandings constructed

about phonemic awareness, or any other of the processes and understandings associated with reading and writing, are always embedded with and
connected with all the other processes operating in concert" (pp. 313–314).
She emphasized that it is the richness of these embedded and intercon-
nected understandings that supports children's literacy learning. Children
who have had many opportunities to learn about reading and writing
through interactions in a variety of literacy events develop a deeper and
qualitatively different kind of understanding than children whose understandings have developed largely through training—especially if that training has focused on the teaching of letter-sound correspondences or other
skills in the absence of a purpose drawn from a larger, meaningful activity.
McGee did not object to the gamelike activities in these training programs
because children, on their own, do play with language. (Also, as described
earlier, children create "phonics exercises" for themselves when engaged in
invented spelling.) What is at issue is the connections made for children
between these activities and their purposeful engagement in the full processes of reading and writing. McGee concluded:

> I would suggest that for children who have not developed a rich, sophisticated
> phonemic awareness—and many children do not—we should instead exam-
> ine our instruction to see whether it does provide opportunities to develop
> these kinds of understandings. If not, we should build more explicit attention
> within the more natural activities. (p. 314)

Continuum of Instructional Approaches

The sixth understanding centers on a continuum of instructional
approaches for promoting students' learning to read during the elementary
school grades. I have observed the use of these strategies in the classrooms
of teachers whose success in promoting the literacy of Hawaiian students
was well documented (Au & Carroll, 1997). These instructional approaches
are presented in Figure 6.2. Two instructional approaches are shown to be
appropriate to all grades: teacher read-alouds and sustained silent reading.
The other four instructional approaches are arranged in the order in which
they would often be judged appropriate, given students' progress in learning to read. Beginning at kindergarten and moving up the grades, these
are: shared reading, guided reading, guided comprehension, and literature discussion groups. The use of these approaches is not linear. Teachers
may use some combination of these approaches with a particular group of
students, for example, adding opportunities for guided comprehension to

Figure 6.2. Continuum of Instructional Approaches

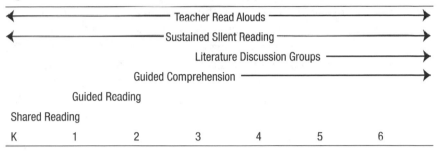

shared reading and guided reading. The nature of the text may also influence the teacher's choice of approach. For example, a teacher may plan to have students engage in a literature discussion group. However, if the novel proves particularly challenging for students, she may decide instead to use guided comprehension, to provide students with more scaffolding.

Although this sequence indicates a rough timeline for many students, there are, of course, those who are progressing more rapidly or more slowly. In most second-grade classrooms in schools in low-income Hawaiian communities, I can usually identify a group of about four students whose literacy is still emergent and for whom shared reading is the appropriate instructional approach at the beginning of the school year. In other words, these instructional approaches are less tied to grade levels and more tied to students' needs in learning to read.

Literature discussion groups. I comment first on literature discussion groups, because this is the newest instructional approach in my repertoire as a teacher educator and the one that caused me seriously to rethink my views of reading instruction. Literature discussion groups may also be called book clubs (Raphael & McMahon, 1994) or literature circles (Short & Pierce, 1990). Literature discussion groups promote students' ownership of literacy by giving them the opportunity to shape their own conversations about literature. Talk does not follow the typical pattern of classroom recitation driven by the teacher's quizzing. Rather, as Atwell (1987) put it, these are "conversations around the dining room table," or in the words of Eeds and Wells (1989), "grand conversations," the kinds of conversations that adults might have in the real world when discussing books with family, friends, and colleagues.

In workshops on literature-based instruction, I try to give teachers the opportunity to engage in such conversations. I begin these workshops by having teachers read and write in response to a poem, then share their responses in a literature discussion group. I always choose a poem that appears to offer room for a number of different yet plausible interpretations. "Riding the San Francisco Train" by Diane O'Hehir (1988) is a good example of such a poem. Readers usually agree that this poem conveys feelings of guilt, but they differ widely in their view of the probable source of the guilt. Participants think that the individual is gay, has just been released from prison, or has left an abusive relationship, and they are always able to support their views by referring to particular lines in the poem. Most teachers are surprised by the extent to which literature discussion groups capture their interest and attention, and they contrast this experience with that of typical school discussions of litera-ture, in which the student's goal is to arrive at the canonical interpretation or that favored by the teacher. This brief experience with literature discus-sion groups often helps teachers gain insights about the differences between literature-based instruction, rooted in reader response theory (Rosenblatt, 1991), and other ways of teaching reading.

Many teachers are quick to see the value of having their students par-ticipate in literature discussion groups. For teachers in the primary grades, the question arises: If students are to gain the background needed for them to participate in and benefit from literature discussion groups, how do we prepare them for this experience? To address this question, I briefly discuss my views of the other instructional approaches in the continuum, begin-ning with shared reading.

Shared reading. Shared reading developed from the shared book experience, as Holdaway (1979) described it. Holdaway had the insight that the benefits of family storybook reading could be brought into the classroom through the shared reading of enlarged texts, or what are now called "big books." As mentioned earlier, many Hawaiian children in low-income communities enter kindergarten without having participated in family storybook reading. Shared reading, in conjunction with the reading aloud of picture storybooks, provides the teacher with a prime opportunity to introduce these children to the joys of reading and of books.

When they enter kindergarten, many young Hawaiian children are in the awareness stage in their development of word identification ability. Shared reading is beneficial because it provides teachers with opportunities to promote all four of the understandings about the relationships between spoken and written language that develop during this stage. Teachers can help children gain knowledge of an important function of print, that print can be used to communicate stories. Teachers can model how readers observe conventions of print, such as directionality. Teachers can call children's attention to the forms of print, including letters of the alphabet and punctuation. Teachers can develop children's phonemic awareness, by pointing out or having children identify words that rhyme, or words that begin or end with the same sounds.

In terms of the development of word identification ability, shared reading serves the crucial function of moving children from paying attention only to pictures to paying attention to print. As Sulzby's (1985) work on young children's storybook reading demonstrated, this shift is a major landmark in literacy development. Teachers worry that children memorize the texts of big books, and they question whether children are actually referring to print. In my observations of young Hawaiian children, I have seen that memorization of the text plays an important role in their development as readers. The ability to associate certain exact words with each page signals their understanding that the text of a book is stable and unchanging. This understanding leads to another, that the memorized words they recite can be matched with the print on the page. Teachers can guide children to slow down their recitation of the text and to point to each word as they say it. In this way, memorization of the big book text contributes to development of the children's ability to track print. At this point, the children cannot yet use letter information to identify words, but they have progressed from attending only to pictures to attending to print.

Even during the introductory stage with a big book, Holdaway (1979) noted that teachers should "induce sound strategies of word solving by encouraging and discussing suggestions, at an appropriate skill level and without unduly interrupting the story" (p. 72). One activity used during rereading is the masking of individual words in the big book. The teacher uses a sliding mask to reveal the letters in the word, one at a time, for the children's study. When teachers unmask words, they model for children how good readers look at each letter of a word in order, moving from left to right. Many teachers copy the text of the big book on sentence strips or word cards. They involve children in activities that require the reading and arranging of the words in pocket charts. A critical feature of all of these activities is the requirement that children attend closely to print and break away from a reliance on pictures. Shared reading lays the foundation for the independence in word identification furthered through guided reading.

Guided reading. A major focus of guided reading is to teach children to use reading strategies—particularly strategies of word identification—independently. A comprehensive treatment of guided reading, based on the research of Clay (1991), is provided by Fountas and Pinnell (1996). As described by these authors, the strategies promoted through guided reading include those for maintaining fluency, detecting and correcting errors, and problem solving with new words.

Guided reading may be introduced when children are moving from the awareness stage to the accuracy stage. While shared reading is usually conducted with the whole class, guided reading takes place with a small group of children whose reading processes are at a similar level. The teacher introduces a previously unseen little book to this small group, and the children read the book on their own with a minimum of help from the adult. The teacher takes great care in selecting the text. It must be difficult enough to allow children to improve their strategies for problem solving with text, but not so difficult that children cannot read it themselves.

For many Hawaiian children, the move from shared reading to guided reading is quite a leap. For one thing, they must track the print on their own, as they are now looking at their own individual copies of the book, not at a big book in which the teacher is tracking the print for them. Also, they are expected to read through a text that has not previously been read aloud to them. I see teachers providing scaffolding as children make the transition from shared reading to guided reading. For example, the teacher may have the children look at her copy of the book. She remains silent but tracks the print as the children read along for a page or two. Then she has the children continue independently in their own books. During guided reading, the central activity is the children's own independent reading of the text. As the children read the text on their own, the teacher monitors their performance. She encourages children's problem-solving efforts and provides assistance as it is needed. Based on her work with individual children, the teacher usually discovers a point or two that could profitably be discussed with the whole group. "Brief detours" is how Fountas and Pinnell (1996, p. 4) described the problem-solving assistance given by the teacher when children need help. They cautioned teachers to be very quick about individual interventions, so that children can immediately return to their efforts at meaning construction with text. This view echoes Holdaway's (1979) concern that the teacher not "unduly interrupt" the flow of the story during shared reading. By conducting a minilesson after the children have finished reading, the teacher can address the points of difficulty identified earlier.

Guided comprehension. As children gain proficiency in word identification, they are able to read more complex texts. These texts include
picture storybooks, such as *Halmoni and the Picnic* by Choi (1993), that
contain such elements as a theme, memorable characters, and a plot with
a problem and solution. These books offer the possibility for in-depth,
guided comprehension, when the teacher uses questioning to sharpen students' understanding of the theme and other story elements and help them
make personal connections to the text (Au, 1992). These lessons enhance
students' comprehension ability and create opportunities for students to
see connections between the texts they read and their own lives.

Teachers at KEEP used the form of guided comprehension known as
the experience-text-relationship, or ETR approach (Au & Carroll, 1997).
Lessons of about 20 minutes are taught to small groups of children, and
the lessons on a particular story usually take from 3 to 5 days. As in guided
reading, these are children whose reading processes are at a similar level.
The teacher selects a text the students will be able to read largely on their
own, on a topic likely to be of interest, and she identifies a possible theme
for the text. In the experience or "E" phase, the teacher introduces the story
and has the students discuss their experiences which relate to the possible
theme. As the lesson enters the text or "T" phase, the teacher has the students read the first segment of the story silently. As in guided reading, she
assists students who encounter a problem while reading. After reading, the
students discuss this part of the text with the teacher guiding discussion
to focus on key points, such as the characters and events, as well as the
emerging theme. The lesson alternates between silent reading and discussion until students have finished reading the text. In the relationship or "R"
phase, the teacher helps the students draw relationships between their own
experiences and the ideas in the story. It is not uncommon for the students
to construct their own theme for the story, rather than assenting to the
theme planned by the teacher (Au, 1992).

The teacher may focus on one or two teaching points near the end of
the 20-minute lesson. As in shared and guided reading, the idea is that skill
instruction should intrude as little as possible upon students' ongoing efforts
at constructing meaning from text. The teacher has the students return to
the text and reread the passage containing the target word, and she and the
students discuss how the word might be identified and what it might mean.
Often, especially as students reach the third grade, they are beginning to
encounter multisyllabic words, such as *ricochet* or *coincidence* that may not
be part of their speaking vocabularies. The need at this point is not usually

for phonics but for other strategies useful in identifying and deriving the meaning of unfamiliar words. One of these strategies is decoding by analogy, which involves comparison of the new word with words already known (Gaskins et al., 1991). Another is the look in, look around strategy (Herman & Weaver, 1988), which involves looking in the word to find a base word and affixes, and around the passage to gain a sense of what the word might mean.

For many Hawaiian students, guided comprehension provides the background necessary for later participation in literature discussion groups. Teachers encourage students to read carefully and thoughtfully, in preparation for sharing their ideas with others. In the process, teachers familiarize students with traditional comprehension skills such as identifying the sequence of events and with literary elements such as character development, flashbacks, point of view, and theme. Students engage in in-depth discussions of literature, under the teacher's guidance, and present justifications for their interpretations. Perhaps most important, guided comprehension can contribute to students' ownership of literacy, as they learn to make personal connections to books and to see that books can have themes of relevance to their lives.

Read alouds and sustained silent reading. In classrooms with Hawaiian students from low-income communities, read alouds serve the important function of allowing teachers to act as literate role models and to convey their own love of books and reading. This function is particularly important in these classrooms, because few such role models may be available to students.

The reading aloud of picture storybooks in kindergarten and first grade, when shared reading and guided reading are the principal instructional approaches, appears to play a critical role in the literacy development of Hawaiian children. The reason is that the majority of texts children can read on their own in these grades are not likely to be high-quality works of children's literature or have many ideas worth discussing at length. Children delight in books with simple but clever texts, such as *Mrs. Wishy-washy* (Cowley, 1990), and these texts help them acquire a sense of what it is like to be a reader, develop strategies for identifying words, and gain confidence. At the same time, the children's development as readers is greatly enriched if the teacher reads aloud picture storybooks, such as *Mufaro's Beautiful Daughters* by Steptoe (1987), which are too difficult for the children to read on their own. Many Hawaiian children will not be able to read such meaty texts independently until they are in the second or third grades. Picture storybooks give the teacher the opportunity to engage children in thoughtful discussions of literature. They allow teachers to encourage comprehension and personal connections to literature at a depth seldom possible with simpler texts. As I have argued, attention to comprehension and other complex literacy processes is required even in the earliest grades.

Teachers effective in teaching reading to young Hawaiian children often put limits on the books that children may read during the time set aside for sustained silent reading (which in kindergarten and first grade is usually not particularly sustained or silent). One first-grade KEEP teacher marked books according to difficulty, giving each book a blue, yellow, or red dot, and the children in her class knew which books they should be reading. The teacher justified her system to me in these words: "The reason I do that is because I don't want them to start working with books and just read the pictures. I know they can read the pictures already" (J. Oshiro, personal communication, March 15, 1995).

This teacher wanted to be sure her students were focused on print. If children were interested in books they could not yet read on their own, they could take these books home and have their parents read them aloud. A similar insistence on students' independent reading of books at an appropriate level of difficulty is observed at Benchmark School, which has a record of success in assisting struggling readers (Center for the Study of Reading, 1991). In both cases, students have a choice of numerous books, but these books must be those that they can read on their own, so that independent reading contributes to students' application of effective reading strategies.

As this overview of the continuum of six instructional approaches shows, Hawaiian students and others of diverse backgrounds are not expected magically to develop the reading ability that will enable them to engage in thoughtful conversations in literature discussion groups and to comprehend, learn from, and interpret text, informational as well as narrative. Rather, students are systematically guided to this point through the conscientious use of instructional approaches, consistent with a constructivist perspective, that enable them to understand the functions of literacy, to identify words and read them in a fluent and accurate manner, to comprehend text, to construct themes, and to develop personal responses to text.

CONCLUSION

I began with a discussion of the concept of balance in literacy instruction, and it seems fitting in closing to return to that concept. My focus has been on skill contextualization as a dimension of balance and on the importance of integrating phonics instruction into meaningful literacy activities involving the full processes of reading and writing. Proficiency is an essential goal for the literacy achievement of students of diverse backgrounds, and knowledge of phonics is, of course, necessary for proficiency in reading. However, the first task a teacher faces with young Hawaiian children from low-income communities or other children of diverse backgrounds is not the teaching of phonics. Instead, the task is to make sure that students are engaged in meaningful literacy activities, so they realize that literacy can serve real purposes in their own lives.

One of the most compelling purposes for reading is the joy of becoming "lost in a book." Another is the understanding of one's own life that can grow from writing personal narratives. Both these reasons are readily grasped by students of diverse backgrounds when they experience literature-based instruction and the readers' workshop and the process approach to writing and the writers' workshop. When teaching classes of preservice teachers, I find it helps to capture these ideas in simple terms. What you are trying to do, I say, is to help your students fall in love with books and write from the heart.

Students of diverse backgrounds readily learn phonics and other skills when systematic instruction in these skills is integrated into the reading of books and the composing of messages that have meaning to them. In short, balanced literacy instruction should give students of diverse backgrounds the best of both worlds: motivation to use literacy in everyday life, for the purposes they set for themselves, and proficiency in the literacy skills and strategies necessary to accomplish these purposes.

FOLLOW-UP ACTIVITY

Think about the approaches to phonics and basic skill instruction in literacy presently being followed at your school or a school you know well. These approaches might range from minilessons taught as part of the writers' and readers' workshops to scripted lessons from packaged programs. What were the reasons for selecting these particular approaches? How effective have they been in promoting students' learning of phonics and other skills? What are the strengths and weaknesses of these approaches? What would you do to correct the weaknesses?

····················
Chapter 7
····················

Negotiating the Slippery Slope: School Change and Literacy Achievement

The growing edge of my research is in whole-school reform in literacy. This work brings together the four Keys to Success necessary for closing the literacy achievement gap. If we accept Key to Success #1, that the problem is complex and requires a multifaceted solution, we know that we must move away from a focus on individual teachers or even small groups of teachers and toward systemic change in an entire school. This is why we must attend to Key to Success #4, which involves creating a schoolwide professional learning community where teachers can work collaboratively toward a shared vision of high levels of literacy for all students. In these schoolwide communities, teachers pull together to construct a staircase curriculum, coordinated so that instruction builds in a consistent manner from one grade to the next. When a staircase curriculum is in place, struggling learners have a chance of receiving the support they need over the years to grow as readers, writers, and thinkers.

It was one thing for me, as a researcher, to have a vision of schools and classrooms likely to be successful in closing the literacy achievement gap, as described in Chapters 3, 5, and 6. It was quite another actually to work collaboratively with educators in schools to make this vision a reality. In this chapter I discuss insights about school reform gained through work with an approach called the Standards-Based Change (SBC) Process. I describe the evolution of this approach from its beginnings with a single school, through its spread to leadership teams at over 100 schools in Hawai'i and scaling up to 10 schools in Chicago. Successful Hawai'i schools progressed through four levels of implementation, with higher reading test scores being associated with the third level.

Although I had expected to see advantages for schools already using constructivist approaches, the difference between successful and unsuccessful schools was not found in the reading program or philosophy favored by the school at the outset. Rather, the difference resided in Key to Success #4, the culture of the school and whether the teachers could come together to form a schoolwide professional learning community, working collaboratively to build the staircase curriculum leading to their vision of the excellent reader or writer.

Within these schoolwide professional learning communities, teachers developed end-of-year targets (grade-level benchmarks) for students' literacy learning. Teachers collaborated within grade levels and departments to provide the instruction that would help students reach these targets. As we worked on instruction to move students toward the targets, we introduced teachers to approaches and strategies emphasizing higher-level thinking with text and building on the strengths students brought from the home, in keeping with Keys to Success #2 and #3.

The SBC Process appears to be a viable alternative for schools ready to break away from packaged programs and one-size-fits-all reforms to focus on developing teachers' expertise. The SBC Process promotes educators' ownership over literacy improvement efforts and encourages teachers to be creators—rather than mere receivers—of curriculum. In turn, teachers promote students' ownership of literacy and literacy learning.

Newspaper headlines from across the United States reflect the turmoil in public education today, with unprecedented demands on schools and educators and higher academic expectations facing even kindergarten and preschool children. These headlines, reflecting the accountability pressures of higher standards and high-stakes tests, are having predictable effects upon education in schools. My home state of Hawai'i is no exception. "Teachers say they're the ones being left behind," stated a headline in the *Honolulu Advertiser*, while the line below read, "Morale low, frustration high among many" (DePledge, 2004).

I believe that literacy researchers can make valuable contributions by working alongside educators in schools at what appears to be a critical point for public education in the United States. In this chapter I discuss my experiences with school change in response to higher standards: how I became involved in this work and the insights I have gained about working at the school level, scaling up the change process, levels of implementation, and student results. Those of us involved with change efforts know that we are negotiating a slippery slope, a precarious situation in which schools, especially those serving high proportions of students living in poverty, may be labeled as failures to be rescued through the privatization of education. For example, the Hawai'i State Board of Education awarded $7.9 million to three private companies to undertake restructuring efforts at 20 schools that failed to meet targets for improved test scores under federal guidelines (Hurley, 2005).

As noted in earlier chapters, my research has centered on issues of literacy instruction for students of diverse backgrounds, those who differ from the mainstream in terms of ethnicity, social class, and primary language. Specifically, I have studied culturally responsive and constructivist forms of teaching, as described in Chapters 3, 5, and 6. A theme running through my work has been the importance of giving students of diverse backgrounds opportunities to engage in higher-level thinking with text and to develop ownership of literacy (see Chapter 5). I spend time in Hawai'i schools nearly every week, and it has been a humbling and distressing experience to observe the rapidly diminishing opportunities for students of diverse backgrounds to experience constructivist forms of teaching. As in other states, many schools in low-income communities in Hawai'i have chosen, or have been required to adopt, packaged programs as a panacea for low test scores (Dillon, 2003).

Still, I see signs of hope. My school change project in Hawai'i is one of several projects in the United States and elsewhere that follow constructivist principles in focusing on teachers and their expertise as crucial to improving students' literacy achievement (for a review, see Taylor, Raphael, & Au, 2011). These projects follow the same principles of support for organizational change, support for individual change, and a focus on balanced, challenging instruction to improve literacy achievement (Taylor, 2005). The success of these projects indicates that many schools may be ready, willing, and able to engage with approaches that invest in the professional development of teachers, rather than buy yet another packaged program. Literacy researchers have an important role in helping these schools engage in long-term change processes that will enable them to bring all students, including those of diverse backgrounds, to high levels of literacy.

I believe this interest in long-term change, centered on the professional development of teachers, is occurring as a result of what Darling-Hammond (2003) calls midcourse corrections to the standards movement. While the shadow of high-stakes testing looms large, many educators in the United States seem to be realizing that quick-fix remedies, such as intensive test preparation or curriculum narrowing, have only a small effect on test scores and rob students of a high-quality education.

My optimism about the possibilities for change in schools comes from work in progress with an approach called the Standards-Based Change Process (SBC Process), developed in collaboration with educators in Hawai'i. The SBC Process guides a school to create a system for improving student achievement through standards, by focusing on a nine-item To Do List (Au, 2006). The To Do List involves teachers in discussing their philosophical beliefs, setting clear benchmarks for student learning aligned with national and state standards, assessing evidence to monitor students' progress toward meeting the benchmarks, and making instructional improvements on the basis of an analysis of this evidence. To date, many elementary schools in Hawai'i have experienced success with the SBC Process, both in terms of students' literacy achievement and teachers' professional development, and my discussion draws on work with these schools. Preliminary work in middle and high schools with the SBC Process indicates the effectiveness of the same principles for improving student achievement and promoting teachers' ownership of change efforts.

Engaging in work with school change has brought about significant shifts in my thinking as a literacy researcher. I have been fascinated by issues of school change since reading Sarason's (1971) classic work, *The Culture of the School and the Problem of Change*. For many years, however, I saw my role as helping classroom teachers improve their literacy instruction—not as bringing about change in the culture of the school. My research on the literacy learning of Native Hawaiian students showed me the importance of the community of learners, central to the success of the readers' and writers' workshops (Carroll et. al., 1996). Gradually, my thinking evolved to the point where I made the connections to teachers' learning and realized that my work should focus on guiding teachers in a school to form a community of learners, or what DuFour (2004) has called a professional learning community. In keeping with constructivist principles, teachers would develop their own literacy curricula, including goals for student learning, assessments, and instruction, in a manner that would build their ownership of the change process.

BEGINNING THE WORK IN SCHOOL CHANGE

My involvement with issues of school change began as a service to schools, not because of a conscious intention to launch a new line of research. Still, I can see in retrospect that this work, aimed at developing professional learning communities in schools, was a logical extension of my earlier interest in developing classrooms as literate communities. In 1997 I received a call from Kitty Aihara, the Title I coordinator at Kīpapa Elementary School in Mililani, a suburban community on the island of Oʻahu. (Title I of the federal Elementary and Secondary Education Act allocates funds to schools serving students from low-income backgrounds.) Kitty asked if I would help her school with its reading curriculum. She explained that, while work on this curriculum had been underway for nearly 3 years, no consensus had been reached about its details and, perhaps more seriously, teacher buy-in remained an issue.

Kitty's invitation provided me with the opportunity to try a new approach to curriculum development. I had seen that classroom teachers, especially in Title I schools, almost always saw curriculum as something imposed by experts, who might either be outsiders, such as university professors, or specialists in their own school or district. Teachers often did not develop ownership of the curriculum because they had not had a part in creating it. What would happen if the Kīpapa teachers were given the opportunity to construct their own reading curriculum?

I had intended to begin with just a handful of volunteers, but Kitty insisted that all the teachers in the school should be involved in the process from the outset. "We're ready for it," she assured me. Of course Kitty knew the Kīpapa teachers better than I did. In the years that followed, remarkable progress occurred at Kīpapa. What came to be known as the Standards-Based Change Process evolved from analyzing what worked at Kīpapa to bring the teachers together as a professional learning community and to move curriculum development forward.

One of the first lessons I learned was that school change must involve all the teachers in the school from the very start. My earlier thought had been that the wise course was to "go with the goers," the logic being that interested teachers will readily make innovative procedures part of their practice, and their success will inspire other teachers to follow suit. I understood after working at Kīpapa that attempting to introduce change by working with just a handful of volunteers virtually guarantees that the effort will fail to spread through the whole school. One reason is that the faculty has instantly been divided into participants and nonparticipants, creating an attitude of distance on the part of nonparticipants that is difficult to overcome. Another even stronger reason is that "going with the goers" often signals that the school's leaders have failed to confront the issues that may be dividing the faculty. These issues need to be addressed and agreements about common ground for moving forward reached, before substantial change can take place. Improvements in students' literacy achievement of the magnitude needed to raise test scores cannot be made by a handful of classroom teachers who work with students for just a year. Students have the best chance of reaching high levels of literacy when all teachers at a school, at every grade level and department, make a strong commitment to the change process and improved instruction.

A second lesson I learned early on is that a school that successfully negotiates the change process must have a Kitty Aihara, an on-site curriculum leader with deep knowledge of the school and its faculty. Now when I begin work with a new school on the SBC Process, one of the first questions I ask is "Who is your Kitty Aihara?" As Fullan (interviewed by Sparks, 2003) reminds us, change in schools is "technically simple and socially complex" (p. 5). I can offer a new school technical expertise in the form of my knowledge of the SBC Process and my experience with its implementation at other schools, as well as background about the literature on school change. However, I don't have knowledge of the social complexities, such as the relationship between the administration and the faculty or the relationships among teachers, that can determine the success or failure of a change effort. Planning SBC Process workshops with the school's Kitty Aihara helps me to address concerns that may be troubling teachers and correctly gauge the timing of moving teachers forward to the next step.

A great deal of emphasis has been placed on the importance of the principal in leading school change efforts (e.g., Portin, 2004). Certainly, principals must be curriculum leaders. In my experience, however, principals are too busy with administrative responsibilities to manage the details of implementing the SBC Process or similar approaches to school change, which are likely to require numerous meetings with teachers, visits to their classrooms, reviewing of products such as rubrics and student anchor pieces, and planning of professional development sessions. This important work is best assumed by a curriculum coordinator or resource teacher who can provide the diligent leadership needed on a daily basis to keep the change process moving forward. This does not mean that the school's Kitty Aihara works alone; schools successful with the SBC Process often have a team or committee assigned to lead this effort.

Although details of implementing the SBC Process need to be tailored to each school, the overall pattern of a school's movement through the SBC

Process is clearly defined by the To Do List and the four levels, as discussed below. I can easily advise a school about what its next steps should be—that is, provide technical expertise—through e-mail messages and phone calls. The main challenge at a school does not lie in figuring out the next steps in the change process but in managing the social complexities. Staff members know that they have more knowledge of these complexities than I do, and they learn to rely on each other and increase their own capacity for moving the SBC Process forward. The SBC Process appears to have staying power because it is managed by a school's own staff, not by an outsider.

SPREAD OF THE
SCHOOL CHANGE PROCESS IN HAWAI'I

One reason for my optimism about the possibilities for change in schools stems from the fact that news of the success of the SBC Process in Hawai'i spread entirely by word of mouth, suggesting openness to a new approach for improving students' literacy achievement. When an approach works well, it generates interest in neighboring schools. From a single school, Kīpapa, the SBC Process spread to other schools on the island of O'ahu, and then to all but one public school on the island of Hawai'i and to two schools on the island of Maui. Teams of teacher leaders in over 100 schools in our state have received 4 or more days of professional development in the SBC Process.

About 50 schools, or slightly fewer than half of all Hawai'i schools involved with professional development on the SBC Process, have shown the ability to sustain the change process beyond 1 to 2 years. These successful schools are members of the Standards Network of Hawai'i. The network brings curriculum leaders from the various schools together for regular meetings at which they receive research updates, learn of progress with the SBC Process at each school, and share solutions to common obstacles, such as finding adequate time for grade levels to meet.

What about the other schools? Almost all the schools that discontinued the SBC Process or failed to make steady progress began participating through projects aimed at bringing about change in clusters of 6 to 42 schools. The problem with working with schools in a cluster, usually as part of a district initiative, is that individual schools are in different places with respect to their readiness for change. Often, district initiatives do not take these differences into account. Some of these schools might have chosen on their own to participate in the SBC Process, while others would have preferred another avenue. However, all schools ended up participating in the same professional development sessions.

A lesson I learned from these larger-scale efforts is that the SBC Process is definitely not the solution for improving literacy achievement at every school. At some schools, staff members hold to the belief that the answer to improving literacy achievement lies somewhere out there—that someone, somewhere, has developed just the right program. In contrast, schools successful with the SBC Process realize that the answer to improving literacy achievement must come from within.

Another lesson I learned, which again bolstered my optimism, is that the success of the SBC Process has nothing to do with the reading program already in place at the school. I had assumed that the SBC Process would have the best chance for success at schools where teachers were working with constructivist language arts curricula. This assumption was reinforced by the fact that Kīpapa and Holomua, the first two schools to use the SBC Process, have home-grown, literature-based reading curricula. What I found instead is that schools can experience success with the SBC Process while using packaged programs, including basals and highly scripted approaches that, at least on paper, allow teachers little room for instructional decision making.

I have learned that I can and should work with schools interested in the SBC Process regardless of the reading program in place, because schools' ability to manage change and improve instruction seems quite independent of the reading program. I have observed in Hawai'i that the same packaged program may lead to improved test scores in one school but fail to yield the same positive results in another school serving a comparable population of students. What accounts for the difference? It is the culture of the school, not the particular reading program, that has the greater effect on teachers' professional development and student achievement (see, for example, Mosenthal, Lipson, Sortino, Russ, & Mekkelson, 2002).

My decision to work on change in schools having all kinds of reading programs came about through necessity. I knew the SBC Process would have limited impact, especially on the literacy instruction of students of diverse backgrounds, if its application were limited only to schools with a constructivist philosophy of instruction. As a researcher, I have studied and found positive effects for constructivist forms of teaching (Au &

Carroll, 1997), and I know that the readers' and writers' workshops offer rich opportunities to build the literacy proficiency and ownership of students of diverse backgrounds (Carroll et al., 1996). But I realize as well that conducting these workshops requires high levels of teacher expertise and many teachers have neither the opportunities for professional development nor the ongoing support needed to reach such levels of expertise.

To guide a school through the SBC Process, I find that I cannot start with the goal of imposing on teachers my own views about literacy instruction, however cherished and validated by research. Instead, I find that change is better promoted if I encourage the teachers to identify the strengths and weaknesses of the school's present reading program and find ways of compensating for the weaknesses. This is not difficult. Usually the reading program has been in place for at least 2 years, and the teachers already know its strengths and weaknesses. For example, teachers at schools using scripted programs typically identify two problems: Students cannot comprehend text beyond the literal level, and they lack the motivation to read. The teachers' analysis creates the opportunity for me to suggest ideas to promote students' comprehension strategies (Raphael & Au, 2005) and voluntary reading. Teachers are receptive to these ideas because they have been presented in response to needs for improved instruction that they themselves identified. In this roundabout way I find myself returning to issues of higher-level thinking with text and ownership of literacy.

SCALING UP THE SBC PROCESS

In 2002, 5 years after its start in Hawai'i, implementation of the SBC Process began in 10 schools in Chicago, under the auspices of Partnership READ, funded by the Chicago Community Trust and directed by Taffy Raphael at the University of Illinois, Chicago. Obviously, Hawai'i and Chicago provide widely differing contexts for school change to improve literacy achievement. The Hawai'i State Department of Education, the only statewide school district, is the tenth largest in the United States, with about 180,000 students and 13,000 teachers. The average poverty level in Hawai'i's public schools is 50% (based on the number of students qualifying for free or reduced-cost lunch under federal guidelines). Chicago Public Schools is the third largest district in the United States, with about 427,000 students and 41,000 teachers—a system two to three times as large as that of

Hawai'i. The average poverty level in Chicago's public schools—85%—is much higher than in Hawai'i. Chicago provided a stern test of the SBC Process, but the good news is that the approach can be effective in urban schools (Raphael, 2010), as it has been in Hawai'i.

The spread of the SBC Process to schools in Hawai'i, and then to Chicago, raises issues of scaling up, a key concern with school change efforts (Coburn, 2003). Earlier, I indicated that many of the schools unsuccessful in the SBC Process were part of change efforts involving clusters of schools. I believe that the SBC Process can be an effective framework for change projects involving clusters of schools, but certain conditions must be in place to increase the likelihood of a positive outcome.

A first condition is that the SBC Process cannot be mandated; each school must have a chance to learn about the SBC Process and to decide for itself whether this approach provides a good match to its situation. For example, the curriculum coordinator at a high-poverty school told me that each grade level had been working to improve writing instruction, but they were having difficulty pulling their efforts into a writing curriculum coordinated across the whole school. She saw the SBC Process as a way to help her school build a coherent or staircase curriculum in writing, and her judgment proved correct. To take a contrasting example, a group of teacher leaders told me that they knew their school could not work successfully with the SBC Process. This school did not have anyone on site to help support the change process and work with teachers in an ongoing manner. There had been a position available, but the faculty decided to hire a music resource teacher to provide the students with extra instruction. This decision may have been important in enhancing arts education in their school, but it meant that work with the SBC Process would flounder from lack of leadership. This example illustrates the kind of decisions made in a school not yet ready to come together as a professional learning community in which the administration and teachers work together toward common goals. These school leaders decided, wisely, that their school should not attempt to implement the SBC Process.

A second condition is that provisions must be in place to provide continuing external support for each school. In Hawai'i a trainer of trainers model—in which teacher leaders are provided professional development on the SBC Process and are expected to guide implementation at their school—has had only limited success. Teachers do not want to be seen as telling other teachers what to do. Change proceeds more smoothly when an external facilitator, such as a district resource teacher or university professor, works with the curriculum coordinator to introduce teachers in a school to the SBC Process. Teacher leaders can then assist their grade levels or departments with various tasks, such as creating benchmarks or classroom-based assessments, which their background in the SBC Process has prepared them to address.

A third condition is that support must be customized to match conditions in each school. In my experience, one-size-fits-all thinking has been one of the downfalls of SBC Process projects involving clusters of schools. For example, a projectwide SBC Process session might address the topic of collaborative assessment conferences that provide teachers the opportunity to analyze student work closely (Blythe, Allen, & Powell, 1999). Collaborative assessment conferences can be one of the most valuable professional development activities in the SBC Process. However, how collaborative assessment conferences are introduced, and the timing of their introduction, almost always needs to be handled differently at different schools. For example, at a school where teachers have experience scoring student work according to their own rubrics, events similar to collaborative assessment conferences are already taking place. In this case, the conferences can simply be introduced as a refinement to teachers' existing practices. In contrast, it may be necessary to delay the introduction of collaborative assessment conferences at a school where teachers have not yet begun the systematic collection of evidence tied to benchmarks. In short, when all three conditions are in place, the SBC Process is likely to be an effective basis for literacy improvement projects involving clusters of schools.

Work with the SBC Process in schools in Hawai'i and Chicago suggests that it can address several knotty problems of practice (Au, Hirata, & Raphael, 2005). The SBC Process can help schools view change as recursive rather than a one-time event. It can lead schools to make the shift from viewing accountability for student learning as an imposition by external institutions, such as the federal government, to a responsibility valued for internal, ethical reasons. It can facilitate development of a coherent curriculum, leading to the vision of the excellent reader or writer who graduates from the school. Finally, the SBC Process addresses the need for focused professional development. Curriculum coordinators in Hawai'i report that teachers need about 8 days per year to work on tasks related to the SBC Process, and they plan accordingly.

Coburn (2003) proposes a sophisticated view of scaling up that goes beyond an increase in the number of schools involved in a change effort. She conceptualizes scaling up in terms of four related dimensions: (1) depth, or the extent to which the change effort affects classroom instruction; (2) sustainability, or the length of time a change effort can be maintained at a school; (3) spread, or the adopting of new norms and instructional principles within classrooms and schools; and (4) a shift in the ownership of reform from external to internal. Documentation efforts underway in Hawai'i and Chicago—including interviews with educators, videotapes of professional development sessions, photographs of classrooms, and field notes—are providing preliminary indications that the SBC Process can be scaled up in a manner consistent with these four dimensions.

FOUR LEVELS OF IMPLEMENTATION

Charting the progress of Kīpapa and Holomua allowed me to see that the SBC Process moves through four levels of implementation at successful schools: (1) initial implementation, (2) three-times-per-year reporting of results, (3) curriculum guides, and (4) student portfolios. I discuss the first three levels below, as these are well understood. The fourth level, student portfolios, is the subject of ongoing study, as it is just being implemented schoolwide by several elementary schools.

Level 1: Initial Implementation

The first phase involves teachers in gaining an initial understanding of the components needed to implement a complete system for improving student achievement through standards. When I started working with Kīpapa and Holomua, I viewed the change process in four parts: goals for student learning, assessment related to monitoring students' progress toward meeting those goals, analysis and presentation of assessment evidence, and implementation of any needed instructional improvements.

These steps built upon earlier work with teachers in the Kamehameha Elementary Education Program (KEEP), as discussed in earlier chapters. I had learned from this work that one of the keys to improving students' literacy achievement was teachers' clarity about end-of-year learning goals or grade-level benchmarks. We found in KEEP that if experienced teachers in high-poverty schools knew the grade-level benchmarks, they could provide instruction allowing approximately two thirds of their students to meet these targets, as indicated by classroom-based assessments of literacy (Asam et al., 1994). Before the grade-level benchmarks were introduced, only one third of the students in these same schools had attained comparable levels of performance as readers and writers.

As I worked at Kīpapa and Holomua, and then with 14 neighboring schools, I found that I needed to be more specific when explaining the components of the system to teachers. For example, teachers found it helpful when I divided goals for student learning into grade-level benchmarks written in teachers' professional language and "I Can" statements written in language understandable to students. I found that teachers needed to understand the distinction between identifying the kinds of evidence they would use to monitor students' progress, such as written responses to literature, and the procedures to be followed in collecting that evidence, such as the amount of time students would be given to complete the task.

In the fall of 2002, through this evolution, I had arrived at a set of nine items. One day I met with a group of resource teachers to plan a districtwide initiative involving a series of five professional development workshops on the SBC Process for teacher leaders from over 40 schools. Sharon Nakagawa, the district administrator and former principal leading the initiative, pointed to the nine items I had written on the whiteboard and asked if that was what I wanted the schools to accomplish. When I nodded yes, she said, "Then call it the To Do List."

As a researcher, I cringed at the linear and directive connotations of the phrase *To Do List*, but I learned over time that Sharon's intuition was correct. Principals, curriculum coordinators, and classroom teachers had grown weary of devoting long hours to strategic plans, vision and mission statements, performance indicators, and other activities related to standards-based education. They had started to resent standards-based education because they found that all of their hard work was contributing neither to improvements in students' achievement nor to a sense of professional accomplishment. I knew that the SBC Process could lead schools to a system for improving student achievement through standards, where teachers' efforts would finally amount to something. Yet I was unwittingly presenting the SBC Process in a manner that did not make its full potential evident to schools.

As a literacy researcher, I had a tendency to emphasize the flexible and nuanced nature of the system. Sharon recognized that this emphasis could

lead educators in the schools to perceive the system as vague and complicated. Now when I introduce the SBC Process at a school, I describe the
nine items in the To Do List, as shown in Figure 7.1, and ask the teachers
to discuss in grade levels which items they already have in place and which
items they need to develop. Teachers still work through the To Do List in a
flexible way, according to their own judgment about next steps, and I can
explain the nuances as they move along. But teacher buy-in to the change
process is made more certain because I have learned to present the SBC
Process in a clear and straightforward manner centering on the To Do List.

Level 2: Three-Times-Per-Year Reporting of Results

The second phase in the SBC Process occurs when teachers arrive at a
regular schedule of collecting evidence of students' progress toward meet-

Figure 7.1. Standards-Based Change Process To Do List

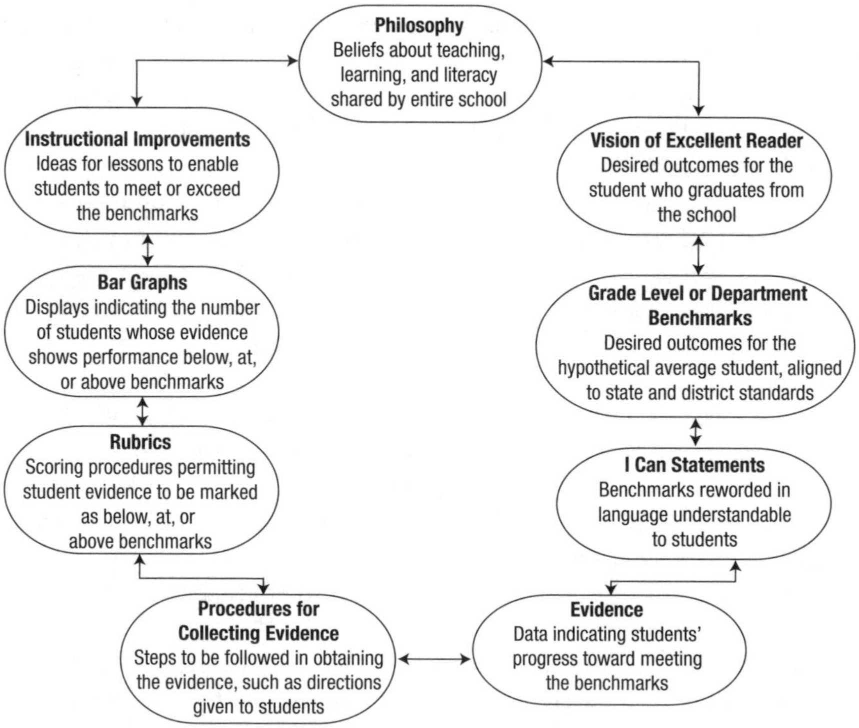

ing benchmarks and reporting their results to the whole school. In the SBC Process teachers collect evidence at the beginning, middle, and end of the year. Schools generally establish 1- or 2-week windows when every teacher will collect evidence for the pretest, midyear check, and posttest. Schools working with the SBC Process are given a template that teachers can follow in preparing their presentations. This template includes all the items in the To Do List, so that teachers can share their grade-level benchmarks, procedures for collecting evidence, rubrics, and anchor pieces.

Sharing this information provides a detailed picture of the expectations for student learning held by teachers at each grade and promotes the school's building of a staircase curriculum, as inconsistencies are identified and remedied. For example, teachers at one grade level will remark to those at another, "We didn't know you were teaching that, but now that we do, we can build on what you've started." Teachers present bar graphs based on the scoring of evidence by rubrics, indicating the number of students who are working on, meeting, or exceeding the grade-level benchmarks. They discuss their analysis of students' strengths and weaknesses and the instructional improvements they plan to implement. Often, they conclude their presentations with reflections on their grade level's progress with the SBC Process, including current issues, such as the need to refine a rubric or develop comprehension strategy lessons. For a school's leadership team as well as for me, these presentations provide information valuable to the tailoring of future professional development on the SBC Process for these teachers.

Many schools enter Level 1 but fail to arrive at Level 2. In my experience, Level 2 represents a turning point because it requires a school to focus on teaching to students' needs as literacy learners, as indicated by the assessment evidence teachers have collected. A substantial number of schools can neither develop nor sustain such a focus. The term "Christmas tree" is used to characterize a school glittering with an overabundance of shiny new initiatives that fragment teachers' time and attention and, in the end, fail to yield improved student learning (Newmann et al., 2001). While the term "Christmas tree school" originated in Chicago, Hawai'i has many such schools as well. Often, the leaders of these schools tell me they cannot afford to set aside the time needed for teachers to work with the SBC Process and arrive at three-times-per-year reporting of reading or writing results because of reasons such as "our math scores are low so we have to work on math," "science is coming up and we have to work on that too," "we're starting a new tutoring program," and so on. When I make it clear that it takes a concerted effort over 2–3 years to see the effects of the SBC Process on student progress, the leaders at these schools tell me that the SBC Process is "too slow" and "we don't have that kind of time." I have concluded that schools unwilling to take the time to arrive at three-times-per-year reporting of results, that lack the discipline to stay the course and focus on what Schmoker (2004) calls "small wins," will almost certainly fail to improve students' literacy achievement.

Level 3: Curriculum Guides

The third level centers on teachers' development of curriculum guides. Although I saw the importance of teachers building the literacy curriculum, I did not foresee teachers actually creating their own curriculum guides as a phase in the SBC Process. I had developed curriculum guides with input from teachers while at KEEP, but I had always thought that classroom teachers would see the organization and writing of the guides as too time-consuming and laborious, given their already busy schedules. Events proved me wrong.

One day, after Kīpapa had been in the SBC Process for 3 years, a small group of teachers went to a meeting with representatives of the three other elementary schools in the area. The other teachers were discussing the reading programs in use at their schools, including basal reading programs and a primary-grade program developed in Australia. They turned to the Kīpapa teachers and asked, "What reading program do you use?" This simple question filled the Kīpapa teachers with dismay, because they did not have a quick phrase to describe their own home-grown, literature-based approach. Kīpapa is the only Title I school in this suburban community, and this fact may have contributed to the teachers' self-doubt. Perhaps, they thought, we should adopt a program at our school.

Kīpapa is a close-knit school, and word spread quickly that some teachers had doubts about continuing with the home-grown approach to reading developed through the SBC Process. Rumors circulated that some teachers wanted to adopt a basal reading program. Certain circumstances contributed to the atmosphere of uneasiness. The principal, a steady force behind the SBC Process, was on medical leave. Kitty Aihara had just retired, to be replaced as the school's curriculum coordinator by Corinne Yogi, an experienced and respected classroom teacher at Kīpapa but new to this leadership position.

Corinne alerted me to the situation, and together we worked out a plan to address it. In two tense meetings, first with the primary teachers and then with the upper-grade teachers, we directly addressed concerns about the direction Kīpapa was taking in developing its own reading curriculum. The turning point of the first meeting occurred when one of the teachers spoke up. She said that she had just discussed the situation with the teacher seated beside her, and that they had no idea why the other teachers were concerned. "We like what we're doing in reading," she declared. Discussion flowed freely after that. The primary teachers noted that their discomfort stemmed largely from uncertainty about what label to give the new approach to reading. In fact, they too favored the home-grown approach to reading and wanted to continue with it. "We'll call it the Kīpapa Reading Curriculum," I said. "The next time somebody asks what reading program you use, you say, 'We use the Kīpapa Reading Curriculum.'" The primary teachers agreed that each grade level would develop its own reading curriculum guide, and we discussed how each guide would have sections for goals for student learning, instructional strategies, instructional materials, and assessment, in keeping with Tyler's (1950) classic principles of curriculum. So far, so good.

After school, I conducted a similar meeting with the upper-grade teachers. Soon these teachers were deep in discussion, weighing the pros and cons of adopting a program versus continuing with their home-grown effort. From my vantage point at the front of the school library, where I stood to guide the discussion, I watched as one by one, the primary teachers silently lined up along the bookcases to see what the upper-grade teachers would decide. In the end, these teachers too agreed to stay the course and to develop their own reading curriculum guides.

That day at Kīpapa taught me that a long-term school change effort needed to do more than involve teachers in a process. The SBC Process also needed to lead teachers to a product, a curriculum guide that would give them something concrete to show for all their hard work. Those who have seen the literacy curriculum guides created by the teachers at Kīpapa, Holomua, and other SBC Process schools are usually amazed by the thought and effort reflected in this work. Teachers who create curriculum guides spend hours and hours on this task and accept the notion that the guides will always be under revision. Development of the guides proceeds quite smoothly because, by following the To Do List, teachers have already prepared many of the materials they need.

When drafts of the curriculum guides are ready, the school holds an event that we call a "carousel," usually lasting about 1 hour. Guides for each grade level are placed on a table in the school library, along with sticky notes that readers can use to leave feedback. Each grade level has 10 minutes to look at the guides prepared by one of the other grade levels. For example, the kindergarten teachers spend this time examining the guides of the first-grade teachers. During the following 10 minutes, they move on to the guides prepared by the second-grade teachers, and so on. Teachers have some familiarity with the work of other grade levels due to the three-times-per-year presentations of results, and this knowledge increases greatly once the curriculum guides have been drafted. Together, the sharing of these presentations and the guides contribute to the development of a coherent, staircase curriculum across the entire school. The close coordination of assessment and instruction across the grade levels appears to be one of the factors contributing to improved literacy achievement at schools working with the SBC Process.

PRELIMINARY RESULTS FOR STUDENTS

The SBC Process aims to improve students' literacy achievement through professional development that empowers teachers to develop their own curricula. The goals of this process are to improve the quality of the educational experience for students and teachers alike. So far, I have referred to evidence of classroom-based assessments, which almost invariably shows growth in students' literacy performance, in areas such as making inferences and summarization, over the course of a school year. However, given the prominence of scores on high-stakes tests as measures of accountability, it is important to ask if the SBC Process might also have an effect on these results.

Case examples suggest that some elementary schools with a strong commitment to the SBC Process, such as Kīpapa in Hawai'i, can see a dramatic rise in test scores (Au, Hirata, & Raphael, 2005). In terms of large-scale analyses, test results for one cohort of students in Hawai'i, fifth graders in spring 2004, have been analyzed using hierarchical linear modeling (Bryk & Raudenbush, 1992). These preliminary findings indicate that the SBC Process has a small positive effect on Grade 5 state reading test scores in high-poverty elementary schools. Test results increase by 2.79 scale score points for every 1-point increase in level of implementation, after accounting for Grade 3 state reading test scores (p = .03). High-poverty schools are defined as those with a higher percentage of students from low-income backgrounds than the state mean of 50%. Of the 90 schools in this category, 33 had participated in the SBC Process; both SBC Process and non-SBC Process schools had mean poverty levels of 59%. The finding of higher test scores was related to the level the school had reached in the SBC Process, as described above (i.e., initial implementation, three-times-per-year reporting, curriculum guides). Years in the SBC Process approached but did not reach significance, suggesting that schools must make definite moves forward in the change process before reading scores improve. While these preliminary results are promising, analyses of scores for additional cohorts will be required before firm conclusions can be drawn about the effects of the SBC Process on results for large-scale reading tests.

CONCLUSION

Since that eventful day of meetings in the library, the Kīpapa teachers and I have discussed how 3 years of hard work on school change was almost lost in an instant. I have come to see this moment at Kīpapa as another kind of slippery slope. Figure 7.2 illustrates the journey of a school such as Kīpapa through the change process, depicted as climbing up a mountain. Before the journey begins, the school stands, with the majority of other schools serving many students of diverse backgrounds, on the plain of failure where poor literacy achievement is the norm. As the school progresses

Figure 7.2. A School's Journey

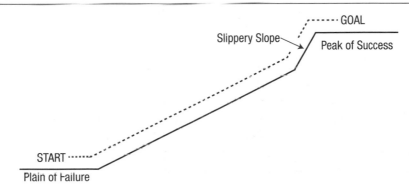

through the change process, it steadily makes its way toward the peak of success, the point at which it can see significant improvement in students' literacy achievement. Danger looms, though, because just before the peak of success lies the slippery slope, the time at which self-doubt is likely to set in. Self-doubt does not occur earlier, because schools lower on the mountain, or at an early level of change, are not yet operating in ways very different from most other schools.

Things are different once the school has made significant progress and nears the peak of success. Suddenly, when asked an innocent question—such as, "What reading program do you use?"—teachers may realize, perhaps for the first time, just how very different things are at their school. They look down at the plain, which they have forgotten was a place of failure, and become aware of their high altitude on the mountain or distance from the norm. Thus, at the very time when the school is closer to the peak of success than ever before, it runs the risk of sliding all the way down to the bottom.

Fortunately, the Kīpapa teachers managed to overcome the slippery slope. During one of our discussions, a teacher extended the metaphor. She explained her insight in words to this effect:

> When we reach the first peak, we're going to say, 'What about that peak over there?' And then we'll be climbing to the top of a new mountain. And there'll always be other mountains to climb. We're never going to be satisfied.

The other teachers agreed that she was correct. This willingness to take on new challenges is the hallmark of schools successful in the SBC Process.

I began with the notion that literacy researchers working on school change are negotiating a slippery slope. I would like to close by referring to the meaning assigned to the phrase slippery slope by philosophers. In the causal version of the slippery slope, it is asserted that if A happens, then by a series of small steps, eventually Z will happen. If Z is a drastic outcome, one that should never be allowed to occur, then A should never be allowed to happen either. Sometimes I allowed myself to slide down this type of logical (or illogical) slippery slope, fearing the worst for a school because it had adopted a certain packaged program. Now I have learned to have faith that, given the opportunity, teachers will see the weaknesses in their instruction and act decisively to make corrections.

One day I attended a meeting for teacher leaders at 14 schools in the SBC Process. First on the agenda was a presentation by teachers from a school that has used a scripted reading program for a number of years. These teachers had found that the program helped their students learn to decode but did little to advance comprehension and motivation to read. They had compensated for these weaknesses with activities such as reading books aloud in class; highlighting a principal's book of the month that was featured in all classrooms; and teaching lessons on how to prepare a written response to literature including interpretations supported with evidence from text. I had been at the school 4 months earlier to get the teachers started with curriculum guides in writing, the focus of the SBC Process in these schools. In their presentation, the teachers shared their writing curriculum guides. The first teacher explained that the guides were "a road map of what we're going to teach." The second teacher stated that, before creating the curriculum guides, she had experienced the feeling that she was working hard but not accomplishing anything. The third teacher described the opportunity to create the guides as "a rewarding accomplishment" and central to the school's development as a professional learning community. All praised their principal for her leadership and for giving grade levels time to work on the guides. The enthusiasm of these teachers for moving their school forward and improving students' literacy achievement radiated through the room. I could see the light in their eyes.

FOLLOW-UP ACTIVITY

Reflect upon the situation in a school familiar to you. Does this school have a schoolwide professional learning community, one that includes all teachers? "All" means encompassing teachers of special education and English language learners. Does this school have a staircase curriculum, extending across all grades in an elementary school or across all grades and departments in a secondary school? If a schoolwide professional learning community and staircase curriculum are not yet in place, what steps could be taken to remedy the situation? What obstacles stand in the way of schoolwide change? How might these obstacles be overcome?

In devising solutions, try to consider all four Keys to Success: (1) devising a multifaceted solution to improving literacy achievement, (2) emphasizing instruction oriented toward higher-level thinking with text,

(3) building on strengths that students bring from the home and community, and (4) creating a schoolwide professional learning community in which teachers work together to construct a staircase curriculum. Refer back to the overall improvement plan you developed in conjunction with the reading of Chapter 2. What revisions would you make to this plan, given what you have learned from this last chapter?

References

Achor, S., & Morales, A. (1990). Chicanas holding doctoral degrees: Social reproduction and cultural ecological approaches. *Anthropology & Education Quarterly, 21*(3), 269–287.

Allington, R. (1991). Children who find learning to read difficult: School responses to diversity. In E. H. Hiebert (Ed.), *Literacy for a diverse society: Perspectives, practices, and policies* (pp. 237–252). New York: Teachers College Press.

Allington, R. (1997, August/September). Overselling phonics. *Reading Today, 15*(1), 15–16.

Allington, R., & Walmsley, S. (1995). *No quick fix: Rethinking literacy programs in America's elementary schools.* New York: Teachers College Press.

Anderson, R. C., Mason, J., & Shirey, L. (1984). The reading group: An experimental investigation of a labyrinth. *Reading Research Quarterly, 20*(1), 6–38.

Applebee, A. (1991). Literature: Whose heritage? In E. H. Hiebert (Ed.), *Literacy for a diverse society: Perspectives, practices, and policies* (pp. 228–236). New York: Teachers College Press.

Armstrong, R. (1858). *Report of the president of the board of education to the Hawaiian legislature.* Honolulu, HI: Kingdom of Hawai'i.

Asam, C., Au, K., Blake, K., Carroll, J., Jacobson, H., Kunitake, M., Oshiro, M., & Scheu, J. (1993). *The demonstration classroom project: Report of Year 1.* Honolulu, HI: Kamehameha Elementary Education Program.

Asam, C., Au, K., Blake, K., Carroll, J., Jacobson, H., Kunitake, M., Oshiro, M., & Scheu, J. (1994). *The demonstration classroom project: Report of Year 2.* Honolulu, HI: Kamehameha Elementary Education Program.

Atwell, N. (1987). *In the middle: Writing, reading, and learning with adolescents.* Portsmouth, NH: Boynton/Cook.

Au, K. (1976). Analyzing oral reading errors to improve instruction. *The Reading Teacher, 31*(1), 46–49.

Au, K. (1979). Using the experience-text-relationship method with minority children. *The Reading Teacher, 32*(6), 677–679.

Au, K. (1980). Participation structures in a reading lesson with Hawaiian children: Analysis of a culturally appropriate instructional event. *Anthropology and Education Quarterly, 11*(2), 91–115

Au, K. (1992). Constructing the theme of a story. *Language Arts, 69*(2), 106–111.

Au, K. (1993). *Literacy instruction in multicultural settings.* Fort Worth, TX: Harcourt Brace Jovanovich College Publishers

Au, K. (1994). Portfolio assessment: Experiences at the Kamehameha Elementary Education Program. In S. Valencia, E. Hiebert, & P. Afflerbach (Eds.), *Authentic reading assessment: Practices and possibilities* (pp. 103–126). Newark, DE: International Reading Association.

Au, K. (2006). *Multicultural issues and literacy achievement*. Mahwah, NJ: Erlbaum.

Au, K., & Asam, C. (1996). Improving the literacy achievement of low-income students of diverse backgrounds. In M. Graves, P. Van den Broek, & B. Taylor (Eds.), *The first R: Every child's right to read* (pp. 199–223). New York: Teachers College Press.

Au, K., & Carroll, J. (1997). Improving literacy achievement through a constructivist approach: The KEEP demonstration classroom project. *Elementary School Journal, 97*(3), 203–221.

Au, K., Carroll, J., & Scheu, J. (1997). *Balanced literacy instruction: A teacher's resource book*. Norwood, MA: Christopher-Gordon.

Au, K., Hirata, S., & Raphael, T. (2005). Inspiring literacy achievement through standards. *The California Reader, 39*(1), 5–11.

Au, K., & Jordan, C. (1981). Teaching reading to Hawaiian children: Finding a culturally appropriate solution. In H. Trueba, G. Guthrie, & K. Au (Eds.), *Culture and the bilingual classroom: Studies in classroom ethnography* (pp. 129–152). Rowley, MA: Newbury House.

Au, K., & Kaomea, J. (2009). Reading comprehension and diversity in historical perspective: Literacy, power, and Native Hawaiians. In S. Israel & G. Duffy (Eds.), *Handbook of research on reading comprehension* (pp. 571–586). New York: Routledge.

Au, K., & Kawakami, A. (1994). Cultural congruence in instruction. In E. Hollins, J. King, & W. Hayman (Eds.), *Teaching diverse populations: Formulating a knowledge base* (pp. 5–23). Albany: State University of New York Press.

Au, K., & Mason, J. (1981). Social organizational factors in learning to read: The balance of rights hypothesis. *Reading Research Quarterly, 17*(1), 115–152.

Au, K., & Mason, J. (1983). Cultural congruence in classroom participation structures: Achieving a balance of rights. *Discourse Processes, 6*, 145–167.

Au, K., & Raphael, T. (2000). Equity and literacy in the next millennium. *Reading Research Quarterly, 35*(1), 170–188.

Au, K., & Raphael, T. (2007). Classroom assessment and standards-based change. In J. Paratore & R. McCormack (Eds.), *Classroom literacy assessment* (pp. 306–322). New York: Guilford Press.

Au, K., Raphael, T., & Mooney, K. (2008a). Improving reading achievement in elementary schools: Guiding change in a time of standards. In S. Wepner & D. Strickland (Eds.), *The administration and supervision of reading programs* (4th ed., pp. 71–89). New York: Teachers College Press.

Au, K., Raphael, T., & Mooney, K. (2008b). What we have learned about teacher education to improve literacy achievement in urban schools. In V. Chou, L. Morrow, & L. Wilkinson (Eds.), *Improving the preparation of teachers of reading in urban settings: Policy, practice, pedagogy* (pp. 159–184). Newark DE: International Reading Association.

Au, K., & Scheu, J. (1996). Journey toward holistic instruction. *The Reading Teacher, 49*(6), 468–477.

Au, K., Scheu, J., Kawakami, A., & Herman, P. (1990). Assessment and accountability in a whole literacy curriculum. *The Reading Teacher, 43*(8), 574–578.

Au, K., & Valencia, S. (2010). Fulfilling the potential of standards-based education: Promising policy principles. *Language Arts, 87*(5), 373–380.

Banks, J. A. (1989). Multicultural education: Characteristics and goals. In J. A. Banks & C. A. M. Banks (Eds.), *Multicultural education: Issues and perspectives* (pp. 2–26). Boston: Allyn & Bacon.

Banks, J. A. (1995). Multicultural education: Historical development, dimensions, and practice. In J. A. Banks and C. A. M. Banks (Eds.), *Handbook of research on multicultural education* (pp. 3–24). New York: Macmillan.

Banks, J. A. (2001). Citizenship education and diversity: Implications for teacher education. *Journal of Teacher Education, 52*(1), 5–16.

Barrera, R. (1992). The cultural gap in literature-based literacy instruction. *Education and Urban Society, 24*, 227–243.

Baum, F. (1903). *The wizard of Oz.* Indianapolis: Bobbs-Merrill.

Baumann, J. F. (1984). The effectiveness of a direct instruction paradigm for teaching main idea comprehension. *Reading Research Quarterly, 20*(1), 93–115.

Baumann, J. F., Hoffman, J. V., Moon, J., & Duffy-Hester, A. M. (1998). Where are teachers' voices in the phonics/whole language debate? Results from a survey of U.S. elementary classroom teachers. *The Reading Teacher, 51*(8), 636–650.

Beck, I. L., McKeown, M. G., Sandora, C., Kucan, L., & Worthy, J. (1996). Questioning the author: A yearlong classroom implementation to engage students with text. *Elementary School Journal, 96*(4), 385–414.

Biemiller, A. (1970). The development of the use of graphic and contextual information as children learn to read. *Reading Research Quarterly, 6*, 75–96.

Bishop, C., & Wiese, K. (1938). *The five Chinese brothers.* New York: Coward-McCann.

Blythe, T., Allen, D., & Powell, B. S. (1999). *Looking together at student work: A companion guide to assessing student learning.* New York: Teachers College Press.

Bourdieu, P., & Passeron, J. D. (1977). *Reproduction in education, society and culture.* London: Sage.

Brock, C. H., & Gavelek, J. R. (1998). Fostering children's engagement with text: A sociocultural perspective. In T. E. Raphael & K. H. Au (Eds.), *Literature-based instruction: Reshaping the curriculum* (pp. 72–94). Norwood, MA: Christopher-Gordon.

Bryk, A. S., & Raudenbush, S. W. (1992). *Hierarchical linear models.* Newbury Park, NJ: Sage.

Calkins, L. (1991). *Living between the lines.* Portsmouth, NH: Heinemann.

Calkins, L. (1994). *The art of teaching writing* (2nd ed.). Portsmouth, NH: Heinemann.

Campbell, J. R., & Ashworth, K. P. (Eds.). (1995). *A synthesis of data from NAEP's 1992 integrated reading performance record at grade 4.* Washington, DC: Office of Educational Research and Improvement, U.S. Department of Education.

Carroll, J. H., Wilson, R. A., & Au, K. H. (1996). Explicit instruction in the context of the readers' and writers' workshops. In E. McIntyre & M. Pressley (Eds.), *Balanced instruction: Skills and strategies in whole language* (pp. 39–63). Norwood, MA: Christopher-Gordon.

Cazden, C. B. (1988). *Classroom discourse: The language of teaching and learning.* Portsmouth, NH: Heinemann.

Center for the Study of Reading. (1991). Teaching word identification [Videotape]. Urbana, IL: Center for the Study of Reading; available through the International Reading Association.

Chall, J. (1967). *Learning to read: The great debate.* New York: McGraw-Hill.

Chall, J. (1983). *Stages of reading development.* New York: McGraw Hill.

Chisholm, I. M. (1994). Preparing teachers for multicultural classrooms. *The Journal of Educational Issues of Language Minority Students, 14*, 43–68.

Choi, S. N. (1993). *Halmoni and the picnic.* Boston: Houghton Mifflin

Clay, M. M. (1985). *The early detection of reading difficulties* (3rd ed.). Portsmouth, NH: Heinemann.

Clay, M. M. (1991). *Becoming literate: The construction of inner control.* Portsmouth, NH: Heinemann.

Coburn, C. E. (2003). Rethinking scale: Moving beyond numbers to deep and lasting change. *Educational Researcher, 32*(6), 3–12.

Cole, M., & Griffin, P. (1983). A socio-historical approach to re-mediation. *The Quarterly Newsletter of the Laboratory of Comparative Human Cognition, 5*(4), 69–74.

Cole, M., & Scribner, S. (1974). *Culture and thought: A psychological introduction.* New York: Wiley.

Collier, V. (1989). How long? A synthesis of research on academic achievement in a second language. *TESOL Quarterly, 23*(3), 509–532.

Collins, J. (1997, October 27). How Johnny should read. *Time, 150*(17), 78-81. Retrieved November 1, 2010, from http://www.time.com/time/magazine/article/0,9171,987253-1,00.html

Cowley, J. (1990). *Mrs. Wishy-washy.* Bothell, WA: Wright Group

Crowell, D. C., Kawakami, A. J., & Wong, J. L. (1986). Emerging literacy: Reading-writing experiences in a kindergarten classroom. *The Reading Teacher, 40*(2), 144–149.

Cummins, J. (1986). Empowering minority students: A framework for intervention. *Harvard Educational Review, 56*(1), 18–36.

Cummins, J. (1994). From coercive to collaborative relations of power in the teaching of literacy. In B. Ferdman, R. Weber, & A. Ramirez (Eds.), *Literacy across languages and cultures* (pp. 295–331). Albany: State University of New York Press.

Cummins, J. (2003). BICS and CALP: Origins and rationale for the distinction. In C. Paulston & G. Tucker (Eds.), *Sociolinguistics: The essential readings* (pp. 322–328). Malden, MA: Blackwell.

Cunningham, P. M. (1991). *Phonics we use: Words for reading and writing.* Glenview, IL: Scott Foresman.

D'Amato, J. (1987). The belly of the beast: On cultural differences, castelike status, and the politics of school. *Anthropology and Education Quarterly, 18*(4), 357–361.

D'Amato, J. (1988). "Acting": Hawaiian children's resistance to teachers. *Elementary School Journal, 88*(5), 529–544.

D'Amato, J. (1993). Resistance and compliance in minority classrooms. In E. Jacob & C. Jordan (Eds.), *Minority education: Anthropological perspectives* (pp. 181–207). Norwood, NJ: Ablex.

Dahl, K., & Freppon, P. (1995). A comparison of inner-city children's interpretations of reading and writing instruction in the early grades in skills-based and whole language classrooms. *Reading Research Quarterly, 30*, 50–74.

Darling-Hammond, L. (1995). Inequality and access to knowledge. In J. A. Banks & C. A. M. Banks (Eds.), *Handbook of research on multicultural education* (pp. 465–483). New York: Macmillan.

Darling-Hammond, L. (2003, February 16). Standards and assessments: Where we are and what we need. *Teachers College Record,* ID No. 11109. Retrieved November 2, 2010, from http://www.tcrecord.org/content.asp?contentid=11109

Delpit, L. (1988). The silenced dialogue: Power and pedagogy in educating other people's children. *Harvard Educational Review, 58*, 280–298.

Delpit, L. (1991). A conversation with Lisa Delpit. *Language Arts, 68*(7), 541–547.

Delpit, L. (1995). *Other people's children: Cultural conflict in the classroom.* New York: New Press.

DePledge, D. (2004, April 18). Teachers say they're the ones being left behind. *Honolulu Advertiser.* Retrieved November 2, 2010, from http://the.honoluluadvertiser.com/article/2004/Apr/18/ln/ln11a.html

Dillon, D. R. (2003). In leaving no child behind, have we forsaken individual learners, teachers, schools, and communities? In C. M. Fairbanks (Ed.), *52nd yearbook of the National Reading Conference* (pp. 1–31). Oak Creek WI: National Reading Conference.

Dole, J. A., Duffy, G. G., Roehler, L. R., & Pearson, P. D. (1991). Moving from the old to the new: Research on reading comprehension instruction. *Review of Educational Research, 61*(2), 239–264.

Dudley-Marling, C., & Searle, D. (Eds.). (1995). *Who owns learning: Questions of autonomy, choice, and control.* Portsmouth, NH: Heinemann.

DuFour, R. (2004). What is a "professional learning community"? *Educational Leadership, 61*(8), 6–11.

Dunford, J. (1999, November 28). Hawaii debates classroom pidgin. *Laredo Morning Times.* Retrieved from http://airwolf.lmtonline.com/news/archive/1128/page11.pdf

Edwards, P. (2009). *Tapping the potential of parents: A strategic guide to boosting student achievement through family involvement.* New York: Scholastic.

Eeds, M., & Wells, D. (1989). Grand conversations: An exploration of meaning construction in literature study groups. *Research in the Teaching of English, 23*, 4–29.

Ehri, L. C. (1987). Learning to read and spell words. *Journal of Reading Behavior, 19*(1), 5–31.

Erickson, F. (1993). Transformation and school success: The politics and culture of educational achievement. In E. Jacob & C. Jordan (Eds.), *Minority education: Anthropological perspectives* (pp. 27–51). Norwood, NJ: Ablex.

Erickson, F., & Mohatt, G. (1982). Cultural organization of participation structures in two classrooms of Indian students. In G. B. Spindler (Ed.), *Doing the ethnography of schooling: Educational anthropology in action* (pp. 132–174). New York: Holt, Rinehart & Winston.

Ferguson, R. (2003). Teachers' perceptions and expectations and the black-white test score gap. *Urban Education, 38*(4), 460–507.

Fitzgerald, J. (1995). English-as-a-second-language reading instruction in the United States: A research review. *Journal of Reading Behavior, 27*, 115–152.

Flack, M., & Wiese, K. (1933). *The story about Ping.* New York: Penguin.

Flippo, R. (1998). Points of agreement: A display of professional unity in our field. *The Reading Teacher, 52*(1), 30–40.

Fordham, S. (1991). Peer-proofing academic competition among black adolescents: "Acting white" black American style. In C. E. Sleeter (Ed.), *Empowerment through multicultural education* (pp. 69–93). Albany: State University of New York Press.

Foster, M. (1989). "It's cookin' now": A performance analysis of the speech events of a black teacher in an urban community college. *Language in Society, 18*(1), 1–29.

Fountas, I. C., & Pinnell, G. S. (1996). *Guided reading: Good first teaching for all children.* Portsmouth, NH: Heinemann.

Freppon, P. A., & Dahl, K. L. (1998). Balanced instruction: Insights and considerations. *Reading Research Quarterly, 33*(2), 240–251.

Friedman, T. L. (2000). *The Lexus and the olive tree: Understanding globalization.* New York: Farrar, Straus & Giroux.

Frierson, H. T., Jr. (1990). The situation of black educational researchers: Continuation of a crisis. *Educational Researcher, 19*(2), 12–17.

Frith, U. (1985). Beneath the surface of developmental dyslexia. In K. E. Patterson, J. C. Marshall, & M. Colheart (Eds.), *Surface dyslexia: Neurophysiological and cognitive studies of phonological reading.* Hillsdale, NJ: Erlbaum.

Gallimore, R., Boggs, J. W., & Jordan, C. (1974). *Culture, behavior and education: A study of Hawaiian-Americans.* Beverly Hills, CA: Sage.

Garcia, G. (1991). Factors influencing the English reading test performance of Spanish-speaking Hispanic children. *Reading Research Quarterly, 26*(4), 371–392.

Garcia, G., & Pearson, P. (1991). The role of assessment in a diverse society. In E. Hiebert (Ed.), *Literacy for a diverse society: Perspectives, practices, and policies* (pp. 253–278). New York: Teachers College Press.

Garrison, J. (1995). Deweyan pragmatism and the epistemology of contemporary social constructivism. *American Educational Research Journal, 32*(4), 716–740

Gaskins, I. W., Ehri, L. C., Cress, C., O'Hara, C., & Donnelly, K. (1997). Analyzing words and making discoveries about the alphabetic system: Activities for beginning readers. *Language Arts, 74*(3), 172–184.

Gaskins, R. W., Gaskins, J. C., & Gaskins, I. W. (1991). A decoding program for poor readers—and the rest of the class, too! *Language Arts, 68*(3), 213–225.

Gay, G. (1983). Multiethnic education: Historical developments and future prospects. *Phi Delta Kappan, 64,* 560–563.

Gay, G. (2000). *Culturally responsive teaching: Theory, research, and practice.* New York: Teachers College Press.

Gee, J. P. (1990). *Social linguistics and literacies: Ideology in discourses.* London: Falmer Press.

Giroux, H. A. (1989). Schooling as a form of cultural politics: Toward a pedagogy of difference. In H. A. Giroux & P. McLaren (Eds.), *Critical pedagogy, the state, and cultural struggle* (pp. 125–151). Albany: State University of New York Press.

Gollnick, D., & Chinn, P. (2008). *Multicultural education in a pluralistic society* (8th ed.). Upper Saddle River, NJ: Merrill/Prentice-Hall.

Goodman, K. S. (1986). *What's whole in whole language?* Portsmouth, NH: Heinemann.

Goodman, K. S. (1992). I didn't found whole language. *The Reading Teacher, 46*(3), 188–199.

Grant, C. A., & Secada, W. G. (1990). Preparing teachers for diversity. In W. R. Houston (Ed.), *Handbook of research on teacher education.* New York: Macmillan.

Graves, D. (1983). *Writing: Teachers and children at work.* Exeter, NH: Heinemann.

Graves, D. (1990). *Discover your own literacy.* Portsmouth, NH: Heinemann.

Graves, D. (1994). *A fresh look at writing.* Portsmouth, NH: Heinemann.

Graves, D., & Hansen, J. (1983). The author's chair. *Language Arts, 60*(2), 176–183.

Guba, E. G., & Lincoln, Y. S. (1994). Competing paradigms in qualitative research. In N. K. Denzin & Y. S. Lincoln (Eds.), *Handbook of Qualitative Research* (pp. 105–117). Thousand Oaks, CA: Sage.

Guthrie, J. T., & Alvermann, D. E. (Eds.). (1999). *Engaged reading: Processes, practices, and policy implications.* New York: Teachers College Press.

Guthrie, J. T., Meter, P. V., McCann, A. D., Wigfield, A., Bennett, L., Poundstone, C. C., et al. (1996). Growth of literacy engagement: Changes in motivations and strategies during concept-oriented reading instruction. *Reading Research Quarterly, 31*(3), 306–332.

Hale, J. E. (2001). *Learning while black.* Baltimore, MD: Johns Hopkins University Press.

Hansen, J., & Pearson, P. D. (1983). An instructional study: Improving the inferential comprehension of fourth-grade good and poor readers. *Journal of Educational Psychology, 75*(6), 821–829.

Harris, V. J. (1992). Multiethnic children's literature. In K. D. Wood & A. Moss (Eds.), *Exploring literature in the classroom: Content and methods* (pp. 169–201). Norwood, MA: Christopher-Gordon.

Hayes, K. G. (1992). Attitudes toward education: Voluntary and involuntary immigrants from the same families. *Anthropology & Education Quarterly, 23*(3), 250–267.

Herman, P. A., & Weaver, C. R. (1988, December). *Contextual strategies for learning word meanings.* Paper presented at the National Reading Conference, Tucson, AZ.

Hiebert, E., & Taylor, B. (2000). Beginning reading instruction: Research on early interventions. In M. Kamil, P. Mosenthal, P. Pearson & R. Barr (Eds.), *Handbook of reading research* (Vol. 3, pp. 455–482). Mahwah, NJ: Erlbaum.

Holdaway, D. (1979). *The foundations of literacy.* Sydney, Australia: Ashton Scholastic.

Hollins, E. R. (1982). The Marva Collins story revisited. *Journal of Teacher Education, 33*(1), 37–40.

Hollins, E. R. (1996). *Culture in school learning: Revealing the deep meaning.* Mahwah, NJ: Erlbaum.

Hurley, T. (2005, May 6). BOE approves $7.9M plan to help struggling schools. *Honolulu Advertiser.*

International Reading Association. (1999). *Using multiple methods of beginning reading instruction: A position statement of the International Reading Association.* Newark, DE: International Reading Association.

Jacob, E., & Jordan, C. (1993). Understanding minority education: Framing the issues. In E. Jacob & C. Jordan (Eds.), *Minority education: Anthropological perspectives* (pp. 3–25) Norwood, NJ: Ablex.

Jordan, C. (1985). Translating culture: From ethnographic information to educational program. *Anthropology and Education Quarterly, 16*, 105–123.

Jordan, J. (1988). Nobody mean more to me than you and the future life of Willie Jordan. *Harvard Educational Review, 58*, 363–374.

Jussim, L., & Eccles, J. (1992). Teacher expectations II: Construction and reflection of student achievement. *Journal of Personality and Social Psychology, 63*(6), 947–961.

Kaestle, C. F., Damon-Moore, H., Stedman, L. C., Tinsley, K., & W. V. Trollinger, J. (1991). *Literacy in the United States: Readers and reading since 1880.* New Haven, CT: Yale University Press.

Kahalewai, M. (2005). *Whose slippers are those?* Honolulu, HI: Bess Press.

Kamehameha Schools, Office of Program Evaluation and Planning. (1993). *Native Hawaiian educational assessment, 1993.* Honolulu, HI: Kamehameha Schools, Bernice Pauahi Bishop Estate.

Kincheloe, J. L., & McLaren, P. (2000). Rethinking critical theory and qualitative research. In N. K. Denzin & Y. S. Lincoln (Eds.), *Handbook of qualitative research* (2nd ed., pp. 279–313). Thousand Oaks, CA: Sage.

Kozol, J. (1991). *Savage inequalities: Children in America's schools.* New York: Harper Collins.

Kua, C. (1999, November 2). Speak pidgin, think pidgin, write pidgin? *Honolulu Star-Bulletin.* Retrieved from www.starbulletin.com

Labov, W. (1973). *Language in the inner city: Studies in the Black English vernacular.* Philadelphia: University of Pennsylvania Press.

Labov, W. (1982). Objectivity and commitment in linguistic science: The case of the Black English trial in Ann Arbor. *Language in Society, 11*(2), 165–201.

Ladson-Billings, G. (1994). *The dreamkeepers: Successful teachers of African American children.* San Francisco: Jossey-Bass.

Ladson-Billings, G. (1995). Toward a theory of culturally relevant pedagogy. *American Educational Research Journal, 32*(3), 465–491.

Langer, J., Bartolome, L., Vasquez, O., & Lucas, T. (1990). Meaning construction in school literacy tasks: A study of bilingual students. *American Educational Research Journal, 27*, 427–471.

Larson, J., & Irvine, P. D. (1999). "We call him Dr. King": Reciprocal distancing in urban classrooms. *Language Arts, 76*(5), 393–400.

Lazar, A. M. (2004). *Learning to be literacy teachers in urban schools: Stories of growth and change*. Newark, DE: International Reading Association.

Lee, C. D. (1991). Big picture talkers/words walking without masters: The instructional implications of ethnic voices for an expanded literacy. *Journal of Negro Education, 60*, 291–304.

Lemke, J. (2006). Toward critical multimedia literacy: Technology, research, and politics. In M. McKenna, L. Labbo, R. Kieffer & D. Reinking (Eds.), *International Handbook of Literacy and Technology* (Vol. Two, pp. 3-14). Mahwah NJ: Erlbaum.

Liston, D. P., & Zeichner, K. M. (1991). *Teacher education and the social conditions of schooling*. New York: Routledge & Kegan Paul.

Lomax, R. G., & McGee, L. M. (1987). Young children's concepts about print and reading: Toward a model of word reading acquisition. *Reading Research Quarterly, 22*(2), 237–256.

Lowrey, J. (1942). *The pokey little puppy*. New York: Simon & Schuster.

Lukens, R. J. (1990). *A critical handbook of children's literature* (4th ed.). Glenview, IL: Scott, Foresman.

Lum, D. (1990). *Pass on, no pass back!* Honolulu, HI: Bamboo Ridge Press.

Lum, W. (1990, Summer). Matrices, paradoxes, and personal passions. *Bamboo Ridge,* No. 47, 5–16.

Mason, J. M., & Stewart, J. P. (1989). CAP early childhood screening/diagnostic tests, pilot version. Iowa City, IA: American Testronics.

McCollum, P. (1989). Turn-allocation in lessons with North American and Puerto Rican students: A comparative study. *Anthropology & Education Quarterly, 20*(2), 133–158.

McCormick, C. E., & Mason, J. M. (1986). Intervention procedures for increasing preschool children's interest in and knowledge about reading. In W. H. Teale & E. Sulzby (Eds.), *Emergent literacy: Writing and reading*. Norwood, NJ: Ablex.

McDermott, R., & Gospodinoff, K. (1981). Social contexts for ethnic borders and school failure. In H. Trueba, G. Guthrie, & K. Au (Eds.), *Culture and the bilingual classroom: Studies in classroom ethnography* (pp. 212–230). Rowley, MA: Newbury House.

McGee, L. M., & Purcell-Gates, V. (1997). "So what's going on in research on emergent literacy?" *Reading Research Quarterly, 32*(3), 310–318.

McKinney, C. (2007). *The tattoo*. New York: Soho Press.

McKnight, J. (1995). *The careless society: Community and its counterfeits*. New York: BasicBooks.

Mehan, H. (1979). *Learning lessons: Social organization in the classroom*. Cambridge, MA: Harvard University Press.

Mehan, H. (1981). Social constructivism in psychology and sociology. *The Quarterly Newsletter of the Laboratory of Comparative Human Cognition, 3*(4), 71–77.

Mezynski, K. (1983). Issues concerning the acquisition of knowledge: Effects of vocabulary training on reading comprehension. *Review of Educational Research, 53*(2), 253–279.

Moll, L. (1990). Introduction. In L. Moll (Ed.), *Vygotsky and education: Instructional implications and applications of sociohistorical psychology* (pp. 1–27). Cambridge: Cambridge University Press.

Moll, L. (1992). Literacy research in community and classroom: A sociocultural approach. In R. Beach, J. L. Green, M. L. Kamil, & T. Shanahan (Eds.), *Multidisplinary perspectives on literacy research* (pp. 211–244). Urbana, IL: National Conference on Research in English and National Council of Teachers of English.

Moll, L., & Diaz, S. (1985). Ethnographic pedagogy: Promoting effective bilingual instruction. In E. Garcia & R. Padilla (Eds.), *Advances in bilingual education research* (pp. 127–149). Tucson: University of Arizona Press.

Moll, L., & Diaz, S. (1987). Change as the goal of educational research. *Anthropology and Education Quarterly, 18*(4), 300–311.

Morrow, L. M. (1992). The impact of a literature-based program on literacy achievement, use of literature, and attitudes of children from minority backgrounds. *Reading Research Quarterly, 27*(3), 251–275.

Mosenthal, J., Lipson, M., Sortino, S., Russ, B., & Mekkelsen, J. (2002). Literacy in rural Vermont: Lessons from schools where children succeed. In B. M. Taylor & P. D. Pearson (Eds.), *Teaching reading: Effective schools, accomplished teachers* (pp. 115–140). Mahwah, NJ: Erlbaum.

Nation, K., & Hulme, C. (1997). Phonemic segmentation, not onset-rime segmentation, predicts early reading and spelling skills. *Reading Research Quarterly, 32*(2), 154–167.

National Assessment of Educational Progress (NAEP). (2009). *2009 Grade 12 Sample Questions Booklet.* Washington, DC: National Center for Educational Statistics, Institute of Education Sciences, U.S. Department of Education.

National Assessment of Educational Progress (NAEP). (2010). *2009 reading assessment: National results for grades 4, 8, and 12 by race/ethnicity.* Retrieved December 14, 2010, 2010, from www.nationsreportcard.gov/reading_2009/

Newmann, F. M., Smith, B., Allensworth, E., & Bryk, A. S. (2001). Instructional program coherence: What it is and why it should guide school improvement policy. *Educational Evaluation and Policy Analysis, 23*(4), 297–321.

Nichols, W., Rupley, W., & Webb-Johnson, G. (2000). Teacher's role in providing culturally responsive literacy instruction. *Reading Horizons, 41*(1), 1–18.

Ogbu, J. U. (1981). School ethnography: A multilevel approach. *Anthropology & Education Quarterly, 12*(1), 3–29.

Ogbu, J. U. (1990). Cultural model, identity, and literacy. In J. W. Stigler, R. A. Shweder, & G. Herdt (Eds.), *Cultural psychology* (pp. 520–541). Cambridge: Cambridge University Press.

Ogbu, J. U. (1993). Variability in minority school performance: A problem in search of an explanation. In E. Jacob & C. Jordan (Eds.), *Minority education: Anthropological perspectives* (pp. 83–111). Norwood, NJ: Ablex.

Ohama, M., Gotay, C., Pagano, I., Boles, L., & Craven, D. (1999). Evaluations of Hawaii Creole English and Standard English. *Journal of Language and Social Psychology, 19*(3), 357–377.

O'Hehir, D. (1988). *Home free.* New York: Atheneum.

Osborne, A. B. (1996). Practice into theory into practice: Culturally relevant pedagogy for students we have marginalized and normalized. *Anthropology & Education Quarterly, 27*(3), 285–314.

Osorio, J. K. K. (2002). *Dismembering Lahui: A history of the Hawaiian nation to 1887.* Honolulu: University of Hawai'i Press.

Ousley, O. (1961). *On Cherry Street.* Boston: Ginn.

Palincsar, A. S., & Brown, A. L. (1984). Reciprocal teaching of comprehension-fostering and comprehension-monitoring activities. *Cognition and Instruction, 2*, 117–175.

Pallas, A., Natriello, G., & McDill, E. (1989). Changing nature of the disadvantaged population: Current dimensions and future trends. *Educational Researcher, 18*(5), 16–22.

Pearson, P., & Raphael, T. (1999). Toward a more complex view of balance in the literacy curriculum. In W. Hammond & T. Raphael (Eds.), *Early literacy instruction for the new millennium* (pp. 1–21). Grand Rapids, MI: Michigan Reading Association and Center for the Improvement of Early Reading Achievement.

Pearson, P., & Valencia, S. (1987). Assessment, accountability, and professional prerogative. In J. Readence & R. Baldwin (Eds.), *Research in literacy: Merging perspectives: 36th yearbook of the National Reading Conference* (pp. 3–16). Rochester NY: National Reading Conference.

Pease-Alvarez, L., & Hakuta, K. (1992). Enriching our views of bilingualism and bilingual education. *Educational Researcher, 21*(2), 4–6.

Peters, C., & Wixson, K. (1998). Aligning curriculum, instruction, and assessment in literature-based approaches. In T. Raphael & K. Au (Eds.), *Literature-based instruction: Reshaping the curriculum* (pp. 261–284). Norwood, MA: Christopher-Gordon.

Philips, S. (1972). Participant structures and communicative competence: Warm Springs children in community and classroom. In C. Cazden, V. John, & D. Hymes (Eds.), *Functions of language in the classroom*. New York: Teachers College Press.

Philips, S. (1983). *The invisible culture: Communication in classroom and community on the Warm Springs Indian Reservation*. New York: Longman.

Phillips, D. (1995). The good, the bad, and the ugly: The many faces of constructivism. *Educational Researcher, 24*(7), 5–12.

Piestrup, A. M. (1973). *Black dialect interference and accommodation of reading instruction in first grade*. Monographs of the Language-Behavior Research Laboratory, no. 4. Berkeley: University of California.

Portin, B. (2004). The roles that principals play. *Educational Leadership, 61*(7), 14–18.

Rampey, B. D., Dion, G. S., & Donahue, P. L. (2009). *NAEP 2008 trends in academic progress (NCES 2009–479)*. Washington DC: National Center for Education Statistics, Institute of Education Sciences, U.S. Department of Education.

Raphael, T. (2010). Defying gravity: Literacy reform in urban schools. In K. Leander, D. Rowe, D. Dickinson, R. Jimenez, M. Hundley & V. Risko (Eds.), *Fifty-ninth yearbook of the National Reading Conference* (pp. 22-42). Oak Creek WI: National Reading Conference.

Raphael, T., & Au, K. (Eds.). (1998). *Literature-based instruction: Reshaping the curriculum*. Norwood, MA: Christopher-Gordon.

Raphael, T., & Au, K. (2005). QAR: Enhancing comprehension and test-taking across grades and content areas. *The Reading Teacher, 59*(3), 206–221.

Raphael, T., Au, K., & Goldman, S. (2009). Whole school instructional improvement through the Standards-Based Change Process: A developmental model. In J. Hoffman & Y. Goodman (Eds.), *Changing literacies for changing times* (pp. 198–229). New York: Routledge.

Raphael, T. , Florio-Ruane, S., & George, M. (2001). Book Club Plus: A conceptual framework to organize literacy instruction. *Language Arts, 79*(2), 159–168.

Raphael, T., & Hiebert, E. H. (1996). *Creating an integrated approach to literacy instruction*. Fort Worth, TX: Harcourt Brace College Publishers.

Raphael, T., Highfield, K., & Au, K. (2006). *QAR now: A powerful and practical framework that develops comprehension and higher level thinking in all students*. New York: Scholastic.

Raphael, T., & McMahon, S. (1994). Book Club: An alternative framework for reading instruction. *The Reading Teacher, 48*(2), 102–116.

Rasinski, T. V., & Padak, N. V. (1990). Multicultural learning through children's literature. *Language Arts, 67*(6), 576–580.

Reason, P. (1994). Three approaches to participative inquiry. In N. K. Denzin & Y. K. Lincoln (Eds.), *Handbook of qualitative research* (pp. 324–339). Thousand Oaks, CA: Sage.

Reyes, M. (1991a, April). *The "one size fits all" approach to literacy.* Paper presented at the annual meeting of the American Educational Research Association, Chicago.

Reyes, M. (1991b). A process approach to literacy instruction for Spanish-speaking students: In search of a best fit. In E. H. Hiebert (Ed.), *Literacy for a diverse society: Perspectives, practices, and policies* (pp. 157–171). New York: Teachers College Press.

Rickford, J., & Rickford, A. (1995). Dialect readers revisited. *Linguistics and Education, 7*(2), 107–128.

Rosenblatt, L. (1978). *The reader, the text, the poem: The transactional theory of the literary work.* Carbondale, IL: Southern Illinois University Press.

Rosenblatt, L. (1991). Literary theories. In J. Flood, J. M. Jensen, D. Lapp, & J. R. Squire (Eds.), *Handbook of research on teaching the English language arts.* New York: Macmillan.

Roser, N. L., & Martinez, M. G. (Eds.). (1995). *Book talk and beyond: Children and teachers respond to literature.* Newark, DE: International Reading Association.

Routman, R. (1991). *Invitations.* Portsmouth, NH: Heinemann.

Sahlins, M. (1995). *How "natives" think: About Captain Cook, for example.* Chicago: University of Chicago Press.

Sarason, S. (1971). *The culture of the school and the problem of change.* Boston, MA: Allyn & Bacon.

Sato, C. J. (1985). Linguistic inequality in Hawaii: The post-creole dilemma. In N. Wolfson & J. Manes (Eds.), *Language of inequality* (pp. 255–272). Berlin: Mouton.

Schmoker, M. (2004). Tipping point: From feckless reform to substantive instructional improvement. *Phi Delta Kappan, 85*(6), 424–432.

Schwandt, T. A. (1994). Constructivist, interpretivist approaches to human inquiry. In N. K. Denzin & Y. S. Lincoln (Eds.), *Handbook of qualitative research* (pp. 118–137). Thousand Oaks, CA: Sage.

Scribner, S., & Cole, M. (1981). *The psychology of literacy.* Cambridge, MA: Harvard University Press.

Seuss, T. G. (1938). *The 500 hats of Bartholomew Cubbins.* New York: Random House.

Seuss, T. G. (1949). *Bartholomew and the oobleck.* New York: Random House.

Shannon, P. (1989). *Broken promises: Reading instruction in twentieth-century America.* New York: Bergin & Garvey.

Short, K. G., & Pierce, K. M. (1990). *Talking about books: Creating literate communities.* Portsmouth, NH: Heinemann.

Sipe, L. (2008). *Storytime: Young children's literary understanding in the classroom.* New York: Teachers College Press.

Sleeter, C. E. (1985). A need for research on preservice teacher education for mainstreaming and multicultural teacher education. *Journal of Educational Equity and Leadership, 5*(3), 205–215.

Sleeter, C. E., & Grant, C. A. (1994). *Making choices for multicultural education: Five approaches to race and gender.* New York: Macmillan.

Smith, L. (1999). *Decolonizing methodologies: Research and indigenous peoples.* London: Zed Books.

Snow, C. E. (1990). Rationales for native language instruction: Evidence from research. In A. M. Padilla, H. H. Fairchild, & C. M. Valadez (Eds.), *Bilingual education: Issues and strategies* (pp. 60–74). Newbury Park, CA: Sage.

Sparks, D. (2003). Interview with Michael Fullan: Change agent. *Journal of Staff Development, 24*(1), 55–58.

Spears-Bunton, L. A. (1990). Welcome to my house: African American and European American students' responses to Virginia Hamilton's House of Dies Drear. *Journal of Negro Education, 59*(4), 566–576.

Spiegel, D. (1992). Blending whole language and systematic direct instruction. *The Reading Teacher, 46*, 38–44.

Spiegel, D. (1998). Silver bullets, babies, and bath water: Literature response groups in a balanced literacy program. *The Reading Teacher, 52*(2), 114–124.

Spindler, G., & Spindler, L. (1990). *The American cultural dialogue and its transmission.* London: Falmer Press.

Spivey, N. N. (1997). *The constructivist metaphor: Reading, writing, and the making of meaning.* San Diego: Academic Press.

Stahl, S. (1997). Instructional models in reading: An introduction. In S. Stahl & D. Hayes (Eds.), *Instructional models in reading* (pp. 1–29). Mahwah, NJ: Erlbaum.

Steptoe, J. (1987). *Mufaro's beautiful daughters.* New York: Lothrop, Lee & Shepard.

Street, B. (1995). *Social literacies: Critical approaches to literacy in development, ethnography, and education.* New York: Longman.

Strickland, D. (1994–95). Reinventing our literacy programs: Books, basics, and balance. *The Reading Teacher, 48*, 294–306.

Strickland, D., & Ascher, C. (1992). Low-income African American children and public schooling. In P. W. Jackson (Ed.), *Handbook of research on curriculum* (pp. 609–625). New York: Macmillan.

Sulzby, E. (1985). Children's emerging reading of favorite storybooks: A developmental study. *Reading Research Quarterly, 20*(4), 458–481.

Tatum, A. (2005). *Teaching reading to black adolescent males.* Portland ME: Stenhouse.

Taylor, B. (1982). A summarizing strategy to improve middle grade students' reading and writing skills. *The Reading Teacher, 36*, 202–205.

Taylor, B. (2005). *Consortium for Responsible School Change in Literacy.* Minneapolis MN: Reading Research Center, University of Minnesota.

Taylor, B., Pearson, P., Clark, K., & Walpole, S. (2000). Effective schools and accomplished teachers: Lessons about primary-grade reading instruction in low-income schools. *Elementary School Journal, 101*(2), 121–165.

Taylor, B., Pearson, P., Peterson, D., & Rodriguez, M. (2003). Reading growth in high-poverty classrooms: The influence of teacher practices that encourage cognitive engagement in literacy learning. *Elementary School Journal, 104*, 3–28.

Taylor, B., Pearson, P., Peterson, D., & Rodriguez, M. (2005). The CIERA School Change Framework: an evidenced-based approach to professional development and school reading improvement. *Reading Research Quarterly, 40*(1), 40–69.

Taylor, B., Raphael, T., & Au, K. (2011). School reform in literacy. In P. Pearson, M. Kamil, P. Afflerbach, & E. Dutrow (Eds.), *Handbook of reading research* (Vol. 4, pp. 594–628). New York: Routledge.

Taylor, D., & Dorsey-Gaines, C. (1988). *Growing up literate: Learning from inner-city families.* Portsmouth, NH: Heinemann.

Tharp, R. G. (1982). The effective instruction of comprehension: Results and description of the Kamehameha Early Education Program. *Reading Research Quarterly, 17*(4), 503–526.

Tonouchi, L. (2001). *Da word.* Honolulu, HI: Bamboo Ridge Press.

Townsend, H. S. (1895). *Biennial report of the Bureau of Public Instruction.* Honolulu, HI: Bureau of Public Instruction, Provisional Government of Hawai'i.

Tse, L. (2001). *Why don't they learn English? Separating fact from fallacy in the U.S. language debate*. New York: Teachers College Press.

Tyler, R. (1950). *Basic principles of curriculum and instruction*. Chicago: University of Chicago Press.

Valencia, S., & Lipson, M. (1998). A quest for challenging ideas and meaningful learning. In T. Raphael & K. Au (Eds.), *Literature-based instruction: Reshaping the curriculum* (pp. 96–122). Norwood, MA: Christopher-Gordon.

Vogt, L. A., Jordan, C., & Tharp, R. G. (1987). Explaining school failure, producing school success: Two cases. *Anthropology & Education Quarterly, 18*(4), 276–286.

Vygotsky, L. (1978). *Mind in society: The development of higher psychological processes* (M. Cole, Trans.). Cambridge, MA: Harvard University Press.

Vygotsky, L. (1987). Thinking and speech. In R. Rieber & A. Carton (Eds.), *The collected works of L. S. Vygotsky: Problems of general psychology* (Vol. 1, pp. 37–285). New York: Plenum.

Walker, A. (1982). *The color purple*. New York: Washington Square Press.

Ward, M. (1948). *Little pond in the woods*. New York: Simon & Schuster.

Watson, K. (1975). Transferable communicative routines: Strategies and group identity in two speech events. *Language in Society, 4*, 53–72.

Watson-Gegeo, K., & Boggs, S. (1988). From verbal play to talk story: The role of routine in speech events among Hawaiian children. In S. Ervin-Tripp & C. Mitchell-Kernan (Eds.), *Child discourse* (pp. 67–90). New York: Academic Press.

Weaver, C. (1990). *Understanding whole language: Principles and practices*. Portsmouth, NH: Heinemann.

Weber, R. M. (1991). Linguistic diversity and reading in American society. In R. Barr, M. L. Kamil, P. B. Mosenthal & P. D. Pearson (Eds.), *Handbook of Reading Research* (Vol. 2, pp. 97–119). New York: Longman.

Wenger, E. (1998). *Communities of practice: Learning, meaning, and identity*. Cambridge: Cambridge University Press.

Wertsch, J. (1985). *Vygotski and the social formation of mind*. Cambridge, MA: Harvard University Press.

Wertsch, J. (1990). The voice of rationality in a sociocultural approach to mind. In L. Moll (Ed.), *Vygotsky and education: Instructional implications and applications of sociohistorical psychology* (pp. 111–126). New York: Cambridge University Press.

Whitin, P. (1990). Language learning through family history. In H. Mills & J. Clyde (Eds.), *Portraits of whole language classrooms: Learning for all ages* (pp. 229–224). Portsmouth, NH: Heinemann.

Wilde, S. (1989). Looking at invented spelling: A kidwatcher's guide to spelling, part I. In K. Goodman, Y. Goodman, & W. Hood (Eds.), *The whole language evaluation book* (pp. 213–226). Portsmouth, NH: Heinemann.

Willis, A. (2002). Literacy at Calhoun Colored School 1892-1945. *Reading Research Quarterly, 57*(1), 8-44.

Wilson, C. (2007, October 31). Pride of Maui's Kaunoa School. *Honolulu Advertiser*. Retrieved from www.thehonoluluadvertiser.com

Wilson, W. (1991). Hawaiian language in DOE unique. *Ke Kuamoʻo, 1*(4), 4–6.

Winograd, P., & Paris, S. G. (1988). A cognitive and motivational agenda for reading instruction. *Educational Leadership, 46*(4), 30–36.

Wixson, K. K., Peters, C. W., Weber, E. M., & Roeber, E. D. (1987). New directions in statewide reading assessment. *The Reading Teacher, 40*(8), 749–754.

Yamanaka, L.-A. (1996). *Wild meat and the Bully burgers*. New York: Farrar Strauss Giroux.

Index

complexity of solution to literacy achievement gap, 1–2, 5–6, 27–50
culturally responsive instruction in, x, 1, 23,
25, 59–69, 70
dimensions of, x
emergence of, ix
evolution of concept, ix–x
focus on higher-level thinking in, 2, 6, 25,
30–32, 57–58, 68, 70, 81, 114–116
Keys to Success, 1–4, 5–6, 27–29, 51–52, 70
major issues in, 3
matching approach to, 62–63
multicultural literature and, 17, 44, 80
professional learning communities and, 3, 132
transition from concept to commitment, x
Multilingual education, 55–56
Mun Fook Shinn, 8

Nakamura, Mrs., 90–92, 97, 101, 104
Nation, K., 120
National Assessment of Educational Progress
(NAEP), 28, 53, 55–57, 76
Native Hawaiian Educational Assessment
Program (NHEAP), 76
Natriello, G., 28
Newmann, F. M., 85, 145
Nichols, W., x

Ogbu, John U., 35, 79, 82–83, 93–94, 96, 97, 100
Ohama, M., 77
O'Hara, C., 120
O'Hehir, Diane, 124
Osborne, A. B., 45, 59
Oshiro, J., 129
Oshiro, M., 102, 143
Ousley, O., 16
Ownership of literacy, 42, 80–81, 91–93, 97–100
assessing growth of, 101–102
benchmarks for, 102
defined, 91–92
leading students to high degrees of, 102–103
as overarching goal of education, 97–100,
111–114
proficiency levels and, 103–104
by teachers of educational programs, 85–86

Packaged reading programs, 85
Padak, N. V., 44
Pagano, I., 77
Palincsar, A. S., 115
Pallas, A., 28
Paris, S. G., 112
Partnership READ, 139
Passeron, J. D., 39

Pearl Harbor bombing (1941), 12–13, 54
Pearson, P. D., 47, 55, 78, 81, 108–109, 115–116
Pease-Alvarez, L., 14, 43
Peters, C. W., 98, 112
Peterson, D., 78
Philips, S., 33, 59, 61
Phillips, D., 29
Phonemic awareness, 121–122
Phonics instruction, 109–110, 111, 114
multipronged approach to, 120–122
timing of, 116–118
Picture storybooks, 127–129
Pierce, K. M., 123
Piestrup, A. M., 61, 79
Pinnell, G. S., 126
Pluralism, 17, 25–26
Portfolio assessment, 18, 47, 91, 101–103, 105,
114, 142
Portin, B., 136
Positivism, 29
Postpositivism, 29
Poundstone, C. C., 83
Powell, B. S., 141
Power relations
collaborative, 36, 39
culture of power (Delpit), 46–47
language and, 14, 72–74, 75, 77, 87
and literacy achievement gap, 35–37, 39, 45,
48–49
Process-product relationship, 48
Professional development, 2, 132, 133–152
Professional learning communities, 2, 132
Purcell-Gates, V., 117, 121–122

Radicalism, 49
Rampey, B. D., 28, 56
Raphael, Taffy, 58, 66–68, 81, 83–86, 108–111,
113, 123, 133, 139–141, 148
Rasinski, T. V., 44
Rationales for schooling, and literacy achieve-
ment gap, 34–35
Raudenbush, S. W., 148
Readers' workshop, 66, 89–90
Reading aloud, 15–16, 128–129
Reading skills, 70–88
books and, 14–17
comprehension research, 21–24, 47–48,
80–81, 98, 115
early reading experiences, 14–17
of grandparents, 11–12
Hawai'i Creole (HC) use and, 70–88
language loss and, 13–14, 43, 57
National Assessment of Educational Progress
(NAEP), 28, 53, 55–57, 76

About the Author

Kathryn H. Au is the Chief Executive Officer of SchoolRise, LLC. An internationally recognized literacy researcher, she was a professor at the University of Hawai'i, where she was the first person to hold an endowed chair in education. Kathy's early years as a teacher and researcher were spent at the Kamehameha Elementary Education Program (KEEP). Her research interests are school change and the literacy achievement of students of diverse cultural and linguistic backgrounds. Kathy is a past president of the International Reading Association and of the National Reading Conference/Literacy Research Association. Kathy received the Oscar S. Causey Award for outstanding contributions to reading research and was elected to the Reading Hall of Fame.